CALLED
TO MINISTER
EMPOWERED
TO SERVE

CALLED
TO MINISTER

• • •

EMPOWERED
TO SERVE

GOD ANOINTS WOMEN AND MEN FOR MINISTRY

MARYANN HAWKINS, GENERAL EDITOR
SECOND EDITION

Warner Press
Anderson, Indiana

Coordinator of Publishing & Creative Services
Church of God Ministries, Inc.
PO Box 2420, Anderson, IN 46018-2420
800-848-2464 • www.chog.org

To purchase additional copies of this book, to inquire about distribution, and for all other sales-related matters, please contact:

Warner Press, Inc.
PO Box 2499, Anderson, IN 46018-2499
800-741-7721 • www.warnerpress.org

The version of "Biblical Precedents for Women in Ministry" that appeared in the first edition of *Called to Minister, Empowered to Serve* was edited and expanded into an article titled "A Biblical Vision: Women in Ministry" published in the *Wesleyan Theological Journal* (Spring 1996). Upon request, that journal article was again edited and updated as a chapter in *Reading the Bible in Wesleyan Ways*, 2004. The chapter that appears in this volume is another version of the original work and is only slightly expanded from the original.

ISBN-13: 978-1-59317-631-0

Printed in the United States of America.

13 14 15 16 17 18 / EP / 10 9 8 7 6 5 4 3 2 1

DEDICATION

To our foremothers in faith, current clergywomen,
and those who will follow.

CONTENTS

ACKNOWLEDGEMENTS

Special thanks to Juanita Leonard and Cheryl Sanders, who insisted that a second edition is needed. I appreciate your encouragement. Thanks also to the women who agreed to author chapters, both for the first and second editions. We are in your debt. Thank you to Anderson University School of Theology for the sabbatical time and to my husband, who allowed me to set up an office in our home library.

Thank you also to Aly Hawkins, who took on this editorial project even when she had bigger projects on her plate. Church of God Ministries and Warner Press also deserve thanks for their choice to publish this work both in electronic and hard copy editions.

The final project is my responsibility, and should you find errors or disagree with an idea or posture, please hold me accountable.

God's best to all who had a hand in bringing this text to reality.

Introduction to the Second Edition

Not long ago I was asked, "Why are you working on another book about women clergy? Haven't we settled that issue in the Church of God?" In fact, we *have* settled the issue theologically and more women are being ordained now than at any time in the last forty years. However, as called and equipped for ministry as these women are, many are not finding a *place* to serve. We are not practicing our theology of equality.

The question of women in ministry leadership is certainly not settled in the broader evangelical church, and what happens among evangelicals spills over into the Wesleyan-Holiness churches. As the Church of God has become, in many areas, a group of decentralized community churches, many of the distinctives of the Church of God have been lost; leadership based on spiritual gifts, rather than on gender or other factors, is just one of these distinctives. The more traditionalist wing of the wider evangelical church continues to prohibit women from pastoral ministry.[1] Elizabeth Glanville, building on the work of David Schaller, provides the model of a continuum for thinking about the various positions on women in ministry. On the far left is Fundamental/Traditional, which practices the exclusion of women in any type of pastoral ministry. The mid-point on the continuum is Complementarianism, which states that men and women have complementary roles; women may serve as church clergy, for example, but not as senior pastors. The continuum's far right finds the Egalitarians, who hold that all are equal and there must be no distinction due to gender, race, age, or social status when it comes to ministry. Egalitarians practice gift-based leadership.[2]

In late 2010 Alan F. Johnson edited a book called *How I Changed My Mind about Women in Leadership*. The book contains

---

1. See the Southern Baptist Convention statement concerning women in ministry, for example, at http://www.sbc.net/aboutus/pswomen.asp.

2. Glanville, "Leadership Development for Women in Christian Ministry."

stories from a variety of evangelical leaders whose views have re-oriented toward an inclusion of women as leaders in the church. (Some of these have arrived at what I would call a complementary focus, with a significant bent toward the affirmation of the pastoral couple.) Dallas Willard, who has long affirmed gift-based leadership, notes three points in his preface to *How I Changed My Mind*:

1. Those *gifted* by God for any ministry should serve in the capacities enabled by their gift, and human arrangements should facilitate their service and provide them opportunities to serve.
2. It is misguided and unhelpful to deal with the issue of women in leadership *in terms of rights and equality alone.* Women have an *obligation* to participate in ministry leadership—an obligation that derives from their human abilities empowered by divine gifting.
3. The exclusion of women from "official" ministry positions leaves women with an impression that there is *something wrong with them.* The issue of women in leadership is not a minor or marginal one. It profoundly affects the sense of identity and worth on *both* sides of the gender line; and if wrongly grasped, it restricts the resources for blessing through the church upon an appallingly needy world.[3]

My own doctoral research affirms Willard's comments. A large number of Church of God women I surveyed noted the encouragement they had received from both male and female pastor-mentors.[4] They also had received encouragement from a majority of credentialing committees. However, most of the survey participants also had been rejected time and again when it came time to candidate for a church. There are many congregations that will not even consider a woman as a viable pastoral candidate. How can that be? This is the Church of God!

---

3. Johnson, *How I Changed*, ebook location 62–99.
4. Hawkins, *Church of God Clergywomen.*

At the end of 2012 I had the wonderful opportunity to attend the Asia-Pacific National Leaders Conference in Dhaka, Bangladesh. Leaders from seventeen countries attended the National Leaders Conference. I asked a number of the women present about clergywomen in their countries and discovered that in many Asian countries women are not ordained—but then again, few men are ordained. While this formalizing step is often ignored, women *are* considered primary pastors in significant numbers. Many of these countries are labeled "closed" to Western missionaries, and yet they are flourishing—perhaps because they value the women God has called to serve.

It is my hope that this new edition of *Called to Minister, Empowered to Serve* will challenge the global Church of God reformation movement to likewise value the many women whom God has called to serve and lead the church. This updated volume begins with a chapter concerning ethics by first-edition author Cheryl Sanders. This chapter establishes the foundation for valuing all persons, loving as God loves. Additionally, Sharon Clark Pearson (New Testament precedents and theology), and Susie Stanley (Church of God historical theology) have updated their earlier chapters. It also contains updates by Arnetta Bailey (African American women in ministry), Kathi Sellers (women in cross-cultural ministry), and Cynthia Mansfield (Latina clergywomen), plus a special chapter by Kimberly Majeski on the four Old Testament women named in the birth lineage of Jesus. As in the first edition, chapter 8 contains stories of God's divine call on contemporary women clergy; these are Adrienne Holmes, Carron Odokara, Shannon New Spangler, Abby Smith, and Jael JieMin Tang. The update of Juanita Evans Leonard's chapter, "Women, Change, and the Church," was completed by the current editor.

Two additional items that are important additions to this volume are an appendix, "Women and Men—Partners in Ministry," a sermon transcript from David Sebastian, dean of Anderson University School of Theology, and a six-session curriculum available as a free download from Anderson University School of Theology.

The curriculum is a companion to this second edition and is ideal for Wednesday evening studies, Sunday school, or small groups. To access the curriculum, visit www.anderson.edu/sot/wim/called.

There has long been a precedent for clergywomen in the Church of God. It is a vital part of our DNA as a reformation movement. This affirmation of gift-based leadership, rather than gender-based leadership, is rooted deeply in our heritage and our theology, as this volume shows. May these stories, rooted as they are in the witness of Scripture and of women called to ministry, help the Church of God practice what we preach: that women and men must be empowered to serve if we are to accomplish the mission set before us by God.

Rev. MaryAnn Hawkins, PhD
Professor of Intercultural Studies
Anderson University School of Theology
Convener, Qara: Church of God Women in Ministry

Introduction to the First Edition

JUANITA EVANS LEONARD

On the occasion of the first National Consultation on Women in Ministry and Missions of the Church of God reformation movement, this book is presented in celebration. This book fills a need for the reformation movement that gave birth to it, for the writers who wrote it, and for you who read it. It provides a much needed encouragement to women and men who are engaged in the difficult task of rethinking mission, redesigning curriculum, and redoing theology and ministry within the context of a Holiness community of faith, a community that has from its beginning in the nineteenth century affirmed and upheld the place of women in ministry.

Throughout the century-old history of the reformation movement, women have given significant leadership as pastors, evangelists, educators, counselors, and cross-cultural workers (missionaries) in North America and in countries around the world. As the twenty-first century approaches, it is fitting to examine the history of some of these women who contributed greatly, not only to this movement, but to the greater church community.

These women represent the diversity of the Church of God. The biblical foundations for women in ministry will be explored. The role that women have taken in cross-cultural missions of the church will be described. In the chapter devoted to this witness, we glimpse how significant the call was and is to those who serve. The relevance of a social ethic to women in ministry will provide the reader with much thought as we look to the twenty-first century. The church must utilize the gifts of ministry that God has given to women and for which they must give an account.

Across America in the late 1970s and 1980s, clergy women of the Church of God began to question the dearth of women clergy in the pulpits of the church. They also raised questions concerning the gifts of women that could be used in the ministries of the church, training institutions, colleges and seminary, and the general program agencies of the church. By far, the most urgent concern was the need for women in the pulpits. In the beginning of the reformation movement, women's participation in ministry was not questioned. Now this concern was being voiced by women who held pastorates and were nearing retirement and by women who had served as minorities in our several colleges, seminary, and agencies. Lay women joined the discussion and prayed for a change in direction.

In the early days of Anderson Bible Training School (1917), now Anderson University, women were studying for the ministry and missions. It seemed imperative in the late 1970s and 1980s that a few women students and professors at the one seminary of the Church of God should begin to pray, write, and talk about women's call to ministry within the Church of God. To this growing concern the 1984 Consultation on Mission and Ministry: "Directions Toward the Year 2000," under the auspices of the Committee on Long Range Planning of the Executive Council of the Church of God, stated its goals for women and the church. The question was not whether women should have leadership in the church or whether women should be ordained, as many faith communities had debated the issue in the 1970s and 1980s. For these leaders, the issue was this: "women are being called, trained, and ordained for ministry, but few are being called to local pastorates."[1] These leaders said that the church must find the way for the congregations to accept the ministry of women in pastoral and other leadership roles in this generation. An estimated 55 percent of the Church of God constituency is comprised of women, and as the life expectancy increases, women will be the majority participants in worship. According to seminary statistics of the past decade,

---

1. Executive Council Report (2000), 9.

enrollment of women in theological studies is increasing. This book does not consider in depth the nature of all the sociopolitical factors; however, the authors do point the way to such studies.

Responding to the consultation of 1984, Anderson University School of Theology accepted the challenge to enable the church by intentionally committing personnel and resources to the goals for women in the whole body of Christ. The Women of the Church of God presented to the seminary an initial gift that facilitated a meeting of eleven clergy women from different areas of the United States. In St. Louis, Missouri, they gathered for the purpose of exploring the questions raised by the 1984 consultation. These participants prayed and studied Scripture, shared their ministerial journeys, dreamed and designed the first Consultation on Women in Ministry and Mission, and outlined this book. The consultation and the book have the advantage of having been conceived out of the collective journey of women in the Church of God ministry/missions.

The authors of this book have known the call to ministry and missions; they have known rejection and triumph; they have known persecution and fulfillment. Above all, the authors say to those who read this volume that there is a history, that there is a story set in motion by the biblical writers and empowered by the Holy Spirit for today and for the next generations. The hope of the authors is that the story we have told will help you, the reader, to be encouraged for the ministry to which God has called you. This book is but a reflection of what has been and what is. The action is still in process. A full history of the women who have given their lives in ministry throughout the first hundred years of the reformation movement is yet to be written. The changing role of women in society and its effect upon the role of women within the church must be explored elsewhere.

Our foremothers have woven a tapestry with a rich pattern. They have passed it on to us in this generation. It is our prayer that the threads we add will encourage and challenge women and men to serve God and all humanity through the power of the Holy Spirit.

> **Juanita Evans Leonard**
> Emeritus Professor of Church and Society,
>   School of Theology
> Anderson University Coordinator of National
>   Consultation on Women in Ministry and Mission

CHAPTER 1

Ethics of Holiness and Unity in the Church of God

CHERYL SANDERS

E thics as a field of study is the analysis of human actions, institutions, and character using norms such as good and evil, right and wrong. Christian ethics evaluates these factors in light of Christian beliefs. Two doctrinal themes of the Church of God reformation movement, holiness and unity, inform our ethics and shape our specific witness to the world as Christians. In this chapter we will examine Christian ethics in the doctrines of holiness and unity and explore the impact of sex and race on the preaching and practice of ethics in the Church of God.

The gospel of John records that, prior to his arrest and crucifixion, Jesus prayed for his disciples. The following excerpt from John 17 reveals Jesus' desire that his followers be sanctified and unified:

Sanctify them by the truth; your word is truth. As you sent me into the world, I have sent them into the world. For them I sanctify myself, that they too may be truly sanctified. My prayer is not for them alone. I pray also for those who will believe in me through their message, that all of them may be one, Father, just as you are in me and I am in you. (John 17:17–21 NIV)

The followers of Christ are sanctified or set apart for sacred use by means of the Word of God. In effect, by heeding and adhering to divine truth as revealed in the Bible, the Christian becomes fit to be used by God. The purpose of sanctification is to qualify believers to be used by God to present a message to the world that will enable others to believe in Christ. Moreover, Jesus' prayer for the unity of the believers signifies his understanding that unity is necessary to establish the credibility of this witness to the world. Thus, sanctification and unity are key elements of Jesus' prayer and God's plan for the mission of the church—namely, to be sent into the world as witnesses of divine truth.

A functional understanding of holiness and unity also undergirds Paul's application of the (Old Testament) Scriptures to the life of the church at Corinth. In his second letter, Paul counsels the Corinthian believers to "come out" and come together as one family under God:

> "Therefore come out from them and be separate, says the Lord. Touch no unclean thing, and I will receive you." "I will be a Father to you, and you will be my sons and daughters, says the Lord Almighty."
>
> Since we have these promises, dear friends, let us purify ourselves from everything that contaminates body and spirit, perfecting holiness out of reverence for God. (2 Cor 6:17–7:1 NIV1984)

This exhortation to holiness and unity is couched in the language of covenant and promise; the believers are set apart to enter into covenant relationship as sons and daughters of God, and a practical response to receiving God's promises is the pursuit of holiness as an act of worship. The text also indicates that sanctification has two irreducible dimensions: social and personal. The social dimension mandates separation from (that is, "do not be yoked together with") unbelievers on the one hand, and unification with believers (that is, with those who are the temple, people, children of God) on the other. The personal dimension requires each individual to guard against contamination of body and spirit.

These and other biblical texts form a firm foundation for the promotion of holiness and unity by the Church of God. The underlying theological assumptions and ethical implications of these doctrines are particularly illuminating with respect to the experience of women and various racial groups within the Church of God reformation movement.

Some Theological Assumptions Concerning the Attributes of God

The holiness and unity tradition in the Church of God derives its importance primarily from a biblical understanding of who God is and what God is like. Although a careful reading of Scripture reveals numerous characteristics of God, seven attributes have been selected for discussion here because they bear directly on the ethical imperative to holiness and unity. They are creativity, love, truth, righteousness, mercy, grace, and holiness.

The first book of the Bible begins with an account of how the world came into being, and identifies God as *Creator*. Although the creation story is told in at least three different ways in the early chapters of Genesis (see 1:1–2:3; 2:4–25; 5:1–2), each story establishes that God created human beings in God's own image as male and female. Thus, the world and those who inhabit it have one common origin as the handiwork of one Creator, who stamped an express self-image on humankind. Both the male and female bear the image of God, and no implication of inferiority or superiority among persons is implied in any of the three accounts. Even in the story of Adam and Eve, the woman is fashioned to be the man's partner or helper, again with no suggestion of subordination in role or function.

The most obvious reason for sexual differentiation, however, is for the purpose of procreation. Sexual difference is not established as a basis for discrimination or exploitation, but rather for the coming together of men and women to be fruitful in reproduction and to complement and support each other as responsible stewards of God's created order. The union that occurs when a man and woman come together in the marriage relationship reflects the oneness of the Creator whose image is borne by the two. Moreover, the mutual attraction that generally occurs between the sexes is God's design to ensure that the human species will continue to reproduce its own kind.

It should be noted that the concept of race as understood today is meaningless in the context of creation. God created one human race. Although there are different nationalities and languages and even colors of skin among the peoples of the Bible, clearly the notion of classifying human beings into separate groups called *races* based on physical traits is an invention of modern anthropology which serves the ideology and politics of racism. The creation accounts never suggest that God intended for human beings to use their points of difference, sexual or otherwise, as a justification for hatred, but rather for unity and fruitful partnership to God's glory.

God is *love*. If we define love as active concern for the well-being of others, then we can view the Bible in both Testaments as a history of God's expression of active concern for the well-being of the human family God created. The love of God is manifest in the many roles God assumes in relation to persons: as Parent, as Savior and Deliverer, and as comforting Spirit. The special appeal of John 3:16, the biblical text memorized by more Christians than any other, is that it simplifies and summarizes the good news of the gospel of Jesus Christ in terms of God's love for the world: "For God so loved the world, that he gave his only begotten Son, that whosoever believeth in him should not perish, but have everlasting life" (KJV). That love is God's fundamental motive in word and in action is apparent in this verse. It certainly provides the rationale for the concept of covenant, that is, the agreement of promise and protection God repeatedly offers to Israel in the Old Testament and to Jew and Gentile alike in the New Testament. Our apprehension of God's love makes feasible our worship, our prayers, and our confessions, because our belief in a loving God becomes our assurance of finding the acceptance and help we need. God's love extends to every creature, without regard to sex or race, yet if God shows any favoritism at all it is toward those whose need is greatest and who feel most urgently the desire for God's active concern. It is impossible to earn or demand God's love on the basis of merit; by the same token, it is absurd to assume that only certain persons or groups are deserving of God's active concern.

Truth is an important attribute of God because God is the source of all truth, and God's Word is true. The truth of God is fully demonstrated in God's trustworthiness; God can be trusted to perform everything God has promised. The Word of God, conveyed through the Bible, interpreted by faithful preachers and teachers, and tested and tried in the life of the believer, reflects the reality and reliability of God. Truth serves as the basis for discerning the purposes of God in human affairs, as opposed to the false designs of the adversary. The Bible introduces the concept of evil in the Book of Genesis; in the encounter between the serpent and the woman, evil is clearly identified with deceit and denial of the truth. In particular, this story illustrates how the fall of humankind into the misery of broken relationships with each other and with God begins with denial of the truth. Relationships between individuals and groups suffer in the absence of truth, and truth-telling is a necessary foundation for human civilization and for human relationships of all kinds. To say that God is a God of truth is to acknowledge that we cannot fully hear or respond to God until we are willing to be absolutely truthful in God's presence.

Righteousness, simply stated, is the predisposition toward making things right. In the Bible, righteousness is nearly synonymous with justice, especially with regard to God, who is the source of righteousness and the ultimate Judge. Indeed, God establishes and exemplifies the divine norms by which words and deeds, individuals, and nations are judged. Righteousness as justice includes such basic notions as fairness and equity. In divine perspective, it implies doing all that is required to uphold what is right: teaching, testing, chastising, avenging, forgiving, restoring. In this regard, both God's wrath and God's love are means by which righteousness is instituted and justice is served. God's righteousness is the ground of our justification, and the terms of the covenant God has devised require us to deal righteously and justly with our neighbor. This stipulation has special significance with reference to the poor and the disadvantaged; to withhold justice from the victims of oppression is to pour contempt on the belief that God is a righteous Judge who exercises ultimate moral authority over all without regard to social or economic status.

In essence, *mercy* is gratuitous compassion, care expressed without regard to claims or rights. As an attribute of God, mercy complements righteousness without supplanting it. If justice rests on the application of norms and standards and the imposition of penalties and rewards, mercy represents God's insistence that all are worthy of compassion, regardless of whatever else may be deserved or merited. An important element of the concept of mercy isthe assumption that God occupies a superior vantage point, morally and otherwise, with respect to humankind, which in the eternal scheme of affairs gives God sole possession of the power and authority not only to judge but also to acquit. Clearly God expects those who receive mercy to show mercy, especially toward those over whom one has authority or advantage. Grace is closely related to mercy, and the word for grace in the original biblical text gets translated into English in various ways, as mercy, loving-kindness, or goodness.

The specific meaning of *grace* as an attribute of God, however, is the willingness to bestow divine favor. Grace, like love, is a divine characteristic that always has an object or recipient. Grace also has a specific objective, which is redemption. Its purpose is to bestow on the recipient the power to please God, most expressly in our manner of dealing with others. Grace is divinity endowing humanity with power to love. Human beings cannot directly emulate or reciprocate God's grace in this sense. Furthermore, it is impossible for us to assume a posture from which we can show favor to God. Rather, the human manifestation of grace is a quality of ease and elegance in doing what pleases God that signifies one's status as a recipient of divine favor. The signs of grace have little to do with sex, race, or economic status; instead, they indicate success in pleasing God.

To be *holy* is to be separate or set apart, and the very concept of holiness derives from the idea that there exists a divine reality that is "other" than everyone and everything that is. Worship is a reverent response to this sense of otherness. Holiness is God's premier attribute; all other attributes are reflections in some way of God's inherent holiness. Creation is the institution and manifestation of God's holy order; love is God's holy will; God's holy word is truth; righteousness is God's holy way; mercy is God's holy compassion; and God's holy power is mediated by grace to accomplish God's purpose in the world. Applied to persons, the terms *holy* and *holiness* denote being set apart for God's service. God's people are holy because God is holy.

Unity and Holiness: Ethics for the People of God

Based on our theological understanding of God's creativity, love, truth, righteousness, mercy, grace, and holiness, we can designate a corresponding ethics for God's people that advocates unity and holiness. The fundamental conviction that directs this constructive process is the belief that to be ethical is to emulate a God who is creative, loving, truthful, righteous, merciful, gracious, and holy.

When God created humankind, God blessed them and spoke the very first commandment to "be fruitful and increase in number" (Gen 1:28). Although the intent of this initial commandment is procreation, the continuing provision God makes for all dimensions of life, both physical and spiritual, issues not only in physical offspring but also spiritual fruit. Thus, for the believer, the life of the spirit is a fruitful existence, and the inevitable by-product of the indwelling Holy Spirit is love, joy, peace, patience, kindness, goodness, faithfulness, gentleness, and self-control (Gal 5:22–23). Our most intimate connection with the One who created us is revealed as the divine creative process continues to replicate positive values and virtues in us. This spiritual fruit is holy because it comes from God, and it serves God's exclusive purposes in our lives and relationships. Yet there is another sense in which the commandment to be fruitful is fulfilled in the life of the believer. The church increases in number as fruitful Christians bear spiritual offspring by evangelizing and discipling persons into fellowship with Jesus Christ. The realization that human beings were created by one Creator and blessed for fruitful partnership with one another leads to the conclusion that, from the beginning, holiness and unity are established as dominant objectives in God's plan for human existence.

While the fact of creation binds us all into one human family, it is love that identifies us as children of God. The covenant relationship God offers requires us to commit ourselves to active concern for others in response to how God has first loved us. All who enter into covenant on God's terms are bound to love one another and to own each other as brother or sister. This notion of love has a quite different basis than the love we are obligated to show to neighbors and enemies without the expectation of return. It is a familial bond with God as the one Parent of a diverse array of siblings of all classes, colors, and cultures. Furthermore, it is a love we ought to expect to be returned, shared, and increased among all those who identify themselves with the family of God. This covenant, which gives form and shape to the church, is itself a commitment to holiness and unity; the sole measure of its validity before God is our corporate and individual record of embracing as family those who share our commitment and reaching out with concern for those who do not.

Love is the validation of our Christian identity, but truth is what authorizes and authenticates it. Since God gave existence to everyone and everything that is, God is the source of all truth and the unity of all knowledge. Therefore, truth brings unity to the body of believers, who are committed to live in its light. Ethically speaking, we are challenged not only to speak the truth, but also to employ the truth in exposing the lies and deception that plague our existence in the world.

Perhaps the most difficult aspect of truthfulness—the reason we often find silence or complicity more comfortable than truth-telling—is our fear of being subjected ourselves to moral scrutiny. In order to promote the truth, we must accept its full authority over every aspect of our own lives. The light that was intended to dispel the darkness should not be obscured by the moral laxity and stubborn self-centeredness of unenlightened Christians. Clearly, the prophetic dimension of the ministry to which we are called is worthless and impotent in the absence of truth. To advocate holiness and unity with integrity, we must ourselves be united in holiness. We must understand that holiness is the practical application of God's truth to our daily living and that unity is the corporate spirit of the children of light.

As an ethical principle, righteousness means conformity to what is right. The root meaning of the word *righteous* is "right way." For Christians, the right way is God's way, as revealed in God's Word. Righteousness includes our attitudes, actions, and motives. In the individual righteousness is virtue; in society it is justice. Thus, individual unrighteousness and social injustice both are manifestations of sin. The manner in which justice is administered, particularly in cases involving the poor and the disinherited, is a sure measure of the "rightness" of a society's attitudes, actions, and motives. Individual righteousness is imputed by grace that we appropriate by faith; none can achieve righteousness apart from God. But social justice occurs not as an act of grace, but when righteous individuals work and advocate for it. One of the most costly moral errors made by Christians throughout human history is to divorce righteousness from justice, deceived by the idea that righteous individuals can tolerate and thrive in an unjust society with impunity and without addressing its evils or attempting in any way to change it. The interests of righteousness and justice are served when holy people unite to pursue God's way in the social order.

Mercy is the initiative taken to relieve suffering or forgive offenses with a primary concern for showing compassion. If justice is blind, mercy has eyes to see, ears to hear, and a heart to feel the pain of another. The imperative to show mercy is based on the fact that everyone benefits from the mercies of God. We show mercy because we have received mercy. Mercy involves taking risks, such as the possibility that an offender will use acquittal as a springboard for further injustice or that merciful acts will foster a debilitating pattern of dependency in those who otherwise might be moved to take responsibility for their own needs. Even greater risks may come into play, however, when we refuse to show mercy in order to protect ourselves from danger or abuse, resulting in hardened hearts bereft of the capacity to care. In any case, justice must be balanced with mercy and compassion administered conscientiously in the fear of God. We must at all costs avoid the moral tragedy of using our zeal for righteousness as a justification for depriving others of needed help. The cause of unity and holiness is helped, and not hindered, by persons who are moved with conscientious compassion in their dealings with those who, for whatever reason, cannot help themselves.

Grace is a twofold gift of God. By grace we receive salvation through the forgiveness of sin and we receive sanctification as empowerment to serve. As beneficiaries of God's grace, the people of God are enabled to choose what is right in order to please God. Just as the graceful athlete or artist effortlessly undertakes a difficult performance with ease and beauty, the effect of grace in the life of the believer is love, mercy, forgiveness, and every good work readily coming forth under the divine unction of God's Spirit. The experience of salvation initiates and unites us into fellowship with all believers who have received God's saving grace; the experience of sanctification takes us beyond initiation to identify as children of God who graciously accept God's complete authority in our lives. Thus, salvation and sanctification can be seen as personal experiences of grace that lead us to affirm holiness and unity as desirable attributes of our corporate life as members of God's church.

Just as holiness permeates and reflects all of the other attributes of God, it ought also to dominate the ethics and lifestyle of God's people. In summary, the norms of holiness ethics, informed by our theological presuppositions concerning God, are: fruitfulness, in a manner consistent with God's original creative purpose for humankind; love, because God is love; truthfulness with integrity; righteousness with a godly zeal for justice; conscientious compassion, always bearing in mind the mercies God has extended to us; forgiveness, in humble acknowledgment that our salvation and sanctification are gifts of grace; and willingness to be set apart for service to God.

In the Church of God tradition, the lifestyle concerns which follow from these norms include personal considerations such as abstinence from addictive substances such as alcohol, nicotine, and other harmful drugs; strict observance of the marriage covenant as the exclusive context for sexual activity; rejection of forms of entertainment that glorify lust and other ungodly passions; and modesty in dress. However, the biblical holiness tradition (which does not directly address drug use and other lifestyle issues peculiar to our times) is centered on ethical standards such as love, truth, justice, and mercy that illumine the "setting apart" of people for partnership with God and with each other in the work of reconciliation and redemption. In this regard, holiness is more than personal piety or quiet asceticism; it is a bold and aggressive witness to the world, energized by a prophetic zeal for righteousness.

Sex, Race, and Sanctification

In view of the ethics of holiness and unity, the privileged status of the white male in the Church of God is called into serious question. If holiness is our method and unity is our goal, then our ethical practices ought to be governed by the fruitfulness, love, truthfulness, righteousness, compassion, and forgiveness that set us apart as the holy people of a holy God. A system that reserves the vast majority of pastoral and administrative leadership positions in the church for white men not only deviates from the principles of holiness and unity but reveals a stubborn allegiance to sexism and racism. Such a system perpetuates itself by providing role models and support networks for white men who desire to serve, in effect excluding and discouraging those who are not white or male from aspiring to be trained and employed as leaders.

The sexist and racist practices within the Church of God are not only in evidence in the pulpits and agency offices, but also in local congregations. Most of our congregations are strictly segregated by race, and effectively limit the roles and influence of female members. To "reach our hands in fellowship to every blood-washed one" is our song but not our practice, because we prefer to embrace those who are of our same race and class. While women may be gladly received into the fellowship, their ministries are often regarded as subordinate and auxiliary to ministries led by males.

Thankfully, some notable exceptions do exist to this pattern of racial segregation and sexist subordination within the leadership and fellowship of the Church of God, but they are too few. The practice of white male privilege not only contradicts our holiness and unity teaching but also reveals what many of our people really believe—namely, that people who are not white or males are inferior and that it is appropriate to judge and discriminate on that basis. The extent to which Church of God people have assimilated the destructive racist and sexist ideas of the society is alarming, especially in view of the fact that we claim to serve a holy and just God. Instead of modeling for the world a community of faith whose witness is enriched and expanded by openness to all the people whom God has called and equipped for service, the Church of God mirrors the blasphemous duplicity of a society that proclaims that all are created equal but excludes certain groups from access to justice and opportunity. This state of affairs is blasphemous insofar as it is grounded in a belief that God favors the white male, who alone bears God's image.

The Church of God reformation movement has not always embraced and practiced the racist and sexist biases of American culture. The nineteenth-century pioneers, zealous in their advocacy of holiness and unity, largely welcomed the full participation of women and African Americans in the body of Christ during a time when racial and sexual discrimination was legally sanctioned and widely practiced by all sectors of the society. Their vision—that the Spirit calls and equips the saints without respect to racial, sexual, or sectarian boundaries—enabled them to reject both racial segregation and sexual subordination as inappropriate practices for God's church. With the rise of Jim Crow segregation in the South, however, and the demise of progressive evangelical feminism in other regions of the nation, Church of God leaders began to accommodate themselves to these shifting currents of social sentiment against African Americans and women. This process of accommodation to the prevailing racist and sexist ethos of American society set the stage for two developments that have shaped the life of the Church of God in the twentieth century: the founding of the National Association of the Church of God and the gradual retrenchment of women from the ranks of ordained ministry.

African Americans organized separate camp meetings and congregations when they were forced out of fellowship with whites. The experience of women has been somewhat different, given the fact that they were excluded from leadership and not from fellowship. Instead of forming separate contexts for ministry and worship, women tended to accept subordinate status within the church, and women leaders largely have been relegated to roles as missionaries and teachers. Black women have been subjected to dual discrimination within the Church of God: As women, they have not had equal opportunity to assume leadership positions in black congregations or within the National Association; as African Americans, they have been prejudged as unfit for leadership in agency offices and for fellowship in white congregations. In ethical and historical perspective, then, the Church of God has retreated over time from a progressive vision of unity and equality in the body of Christ to a reactionary conformity to the discriminatory divisiveness of our society.

The hurts experienced by women and members of racial groups who have been denied full partnership within the body of Christ will remain unhealed as long as the Church of God continues to accommodate itself to a sexist and racist society. The ignorant insensitivity of persons who have perpetuated exclusivity within the church will, if left unchecked, continue to foster division and strife within the church. As a remedy, the redeemed must re-examine the second blessing in light of the ethics of holiness and unity.

Sanctification is more than pious adherence to a select list of dos and don'ts; it is covenantal empowerment to serve God. The doctrine of sanctification proclaims that by the grace of God we can live free from sin. Our understanding of the sin from which we have been delivered, however, tends to be much too narrow, if measured by the degree of segregation and discrimination that exists within our congregations and national organizations. Since sin is manifested both in personal and social matters, so our sanctification from sin has both personal and social effects. To attend to personal concerns such as sexuality and dress without at the same time acknowledging our responsibility to overcome sin in the social order (for example, racism, sexism, economic exploitation) is to assume the same dubious moral posture as the scribes and Pharisees whom Jesus rebuked by saying:

> You give to God one tenth even of the seasoning herbs, such as mint, dill, and cumin, but you neglect to obey the really important teachings of the Law, such as justice and mercy and honesty. These you should practice, without neglecting the others. (Matt 23:23 TEV)

When more individuals and congregations within the Church of God begin to take seriously the relationship between sanctification and social change, then the barriers of sexual and racial division will be dismantled, much-needed healing and reconciliation will take place, and exciting new applications of the ethics of holiness and unity to the divine task of united ministry to a divided world will emerge.

We will conclude this chapter with a few suggestions for how the ethical norms that reflect our commitment to holiness and unity can redirect our responses to sexual and racial diversity within the Church of God.

The fruitfulness to which we have been called by a creative God begins with men and women coming together as faithful partners and good stewards of God's creation. Our congregations will grow spiritually and numerically if we faithfully model and promote the quality of partnership in ministry and service that celebrates diversity in the pursuit of unity.

We are identified as Christians by our love. One way of expressing our love as active concern is by evangelism that openly encourages persons of both sexes and all races to enter into covenant relationship as one family of one God.

Our witness to the world is authenticated by our commitment to truth, but there can be little integrity in a church that compromises God's truth by complicity with racial and sexual discrimination. Since sin entered the world by the denial of the truth, reconciliation can begin when we take the bold step of speaking the truth in love.

The servants of a just and righteous God must be consistent in our own just action and righteous living. How we apply justice in our organizational and institutional life is a critical measure of our righteousness. We must make every effort to be fair and impartial in our decisions, without being swayed by racial or sexual prejudices. We must always bear in mind that God judges individuals according to one standard of righteousness and judges nations by the administration of justice to the poor and disinherited.

Ministries of mercy and compassion are greatly needed within the church, particularly ministries directed toward women and children who have been hurt by poverty, discrimination, and abuse. The task of ushering whites from racial insensitivity to acceptance requires a special quality of compassion, as does the complementary task of offering healing to those who have been the victims of racist acts and attitudes.

Closely related to the need for mercy is the need for means of offering and receiving forgiveness in the church. By our acceptance of God's grace, we are saved and sanctified. However, the saints must be reminded from time to time that the church is a forgiving community and that we must allow grace to bring forth the spiritual fruit in our lives that will bless others in turn. Genuine unity among persons of different sexes, classes, and cultures is only made possible by grace.

Our testimony of holiness can be totally invalidated by the practice of prejudice. Being set apart for God's exclusive use means that we resist conformity to worldly standards that devalue others on the basis of race and sex, and we reject all forms of discrimination and oppression. Thus, the personal transformation we experience as sanctification also fits us for engagement in social change. May our quest for unity and holiness be fulfilled in the witness of women and men from all racial groups coming to voice as agents of reconciliation.

About the Author

Cheryl Sanders is an ordained minister of the Church of God and currently serves as senior pastor of Third Street Church of God in Washington, DC. She is professor of Christian ethics at Howard University School of Divinity. Her bachelor's degree in mathematics and black studies is from Swarthmore College. She holds the master of divinity degree *cum laude* and the doctor of theology degree in applied theology from Harvard Divinity School. She has been awarded honorary doctor of divinity degrees by Anderson University and Asbury University.

Sanders is the author of several books, including *Ministry at the Margins, Saints in Exile,* and *Empowerment Ethics for a Liberated People.* Her writing has appeared in numerous professional journals and publications, such as the *African American Pulpit,* the *Christian Century, Christianity Today, Journal of Religious Thought, Leadership,* and *Wesleyan Theological Journal.* She was selected to participate in the Institute of Ecumenics in Dossey, Switzerland, where she led a group on "Teaching the Bible in Ecumenical Perspective." In addition to preaching weekly at Third Street Church of God, she has preached at churches, campuses, conferences, and conventions at home and abroad. Her sermons have been published in print and online.

She has taught and lectured at Anderson School of Theology, Clark-Atlanta University, Duke Divinity School, Lutheran Theological Seminary at Gettysburg, Princeton Theological Seminary, Regent University, Shaw University, University of Virginia, Wesley Theological Seminary, and many other colleges, universities, and seminaries throughout the United States. Her major fields of research and teaching include African American religious studies, bio-medical ethics, Christian social ethics, feminist theology, homiletics, and womanist ethics.

CHAPTER 2

Foremothers of the Messiah

BY KIMBERLY MAJESKI

In the pages of the Hebrew Bible, we find stories of women who went before us and left their mark on our history with God. In the material known to us today as the Old Testament, we read of women who were prophets, military leaders, priests, wise women, and wisdom personified. However, to study the lives of these women is no easy task. The stories as we have them were not handed down to us from the women themselves; rather, what we have is an image-rich narrative developed from a covenantal history, drawn on the map of patriarchy. The narratives are primarily concerned with the public lives of men who were in some way related to the patriarchs or were connected to the emergence of the ancient Israelite monarchy. The narratives themselves were also recorded, copied, edited, and compiled by men who lived many centuries after the women and men whose stories are found in the pages of the Bible.

The material we have in our Old Testament existed first as oral tradition in communities that were formed around story; these stories endured across the generations, eventually to be recorded in the codices which are now considered canonical by persons of Jewish and Christian faith. To do the stories of these women justice, we must unearth information about their world, status, society, and gender roles in ancient Israel. Archaeology and anthropological studies, considered in concert with the Scriptures, help us gain a clearer picture of life in ancient Israel for women.

In the Hebrew Bible, we find the stories of a people who traversed the land of the ancient Near East for more than 1,200 years. Of the 1,426 persons named in the narrative of the Old Testament, 111 are women.[1] While this may seem like a small number, the witness of their lives is powerful and their presence in this male-dominated text is—and should be—remarkable. Though a casual reading of the Old Testament might leave us with the impression that women were confined to the home and their sole contribution to God's people was procreation, a closer look demonstrates another dynamic. Mayer Gruber points out that women served as judges (Judg 4:4–5), officiated funerals as clergy (Jer 9:16–19; 2 Chron 35:25), slaughtered animals in priestly and domestic rites, served as prophetesses and sages (2 Sam 14; 20:16–22), and nursed children and read Scripture in public settings.[2] We have accounts of women who served as priestesses (Ex 38:8; 1 Sam 2:22), poets (Ex 15:21; Judg 5:1–31; Prov 31:1–9), musicians (Ps 68:26), "queens, midwives; wet-nurses; babysitters; business persons; scribes; cooks; bakers; producers of cosmetics (1 Sam. 8:13) as well as innkeepers and prostitutes (Josh. 2)."[3]

While the scope of this study will not allow us to consider each of the 111 named women of the Hebrew Bible, we will get to know a representative group and trace their lives, communal impact, and covenantal significance. We do this in an effort to illuminate the

---

1. Murphy, "Women and the Bible," 42.
2. Gruber, "Status of Women in Ancient Judaism," 151.
3. Ibid., 152.

reality that God was active, present, and powerful in the lives of women, reverberating from them, through the nation of Israel, for the good of the world. The women we will consider here are named in the genealogy of Jesus offered in Matthew's gospel. Each of these women emerge from the male-dominated story of ancient Israel, yet their contributions to the story endure into the New Testament canon and beyond. The narratives of these women—Tamar, Rahab, Ruth, and Bathsheba—are, at the most basic level, portraits of women who were significant to the life of ancient Israel; they also offer to us, however, vivid models of women who were agents of God's covenantal and universal work. These models can guide and inspire us today as we too serve as agents of God's covenant.

Tamar

The story of Tamar is found in the middle of the Joseph narrative in Genesis 38. The grand Joseph epoch digresses to a narrative thread concerning Judah, one of Joseph's brothers and Jacob's sons. After marrying a Canaanite woman who bears him three sons, Judah takes a wife, Tamar, for his eldest son, Er (vv 1–6). Upon Er's unfortunate death, Tamar, who is childless, is given as a wife to his younger brother, Onan. This practice is known as Levirate marriage (Deut 25:56). According to Eryl Davies, the primary reason for Levirate marriage among Hebrews was to provide a male issue for the deceased.[4] For the Hebrews, it was vital for a man to continue his lineage by producing offspring. As can be gleaned from countless instances in the Old Testament, there were other means of doing so, such as through adoption and polygamous marriage.[5] In instances when a man died before securing an heir, the Levirate arrangement ensured the continuation of his line. The practice was crucial in a patriarchal society for the preservation of a childless widow as well as for the transfer of inheritance; in ancient Israel, as in other ancient Near Eastern cultures, property was handed down from father to eldest son.

---

4. Davies, "Inheritance Rights," 139.
5. Ibid., 141.

In the Judah-Tamar narrative, Onan is instructed to provide Tamar with a child; Onan subverts his duty, however, and is deemed "wicked" in the sight of the Lord (vv 8–10). Judah is then reluctant to give Tamar to his third son, who is yet too young for marriage, and he instead sends her back to the home of her father (v 11).

The society of ancient Israel was both "patrilocal" and "patrilinear."[6] In a patrilocal society, women move from the homes of their fathers to the homes of their husbands. In a patrilinear society, fathers designate natural or adopted male sons—never daughters—as heirs.[7] Without son or husband, women thus depended on their natal households. When Tamar finds herself without a male heir and without a husband and is sent back to her father's house, she is rendered a desolate woman. Judah instructs Tamar to remain in her father's household until his youngest son, Shelah, is old enough to fulfill his Levirate obligation (v 10). However, Judah fears for his third son's life and keeps him from Tamar after Shelah is old enough to marry, thereby denying his daughter-in-law the right to have a child. But Tamar takes the matter into her own hands (vv 12–14).

Veiled and cloaked so that her identity will not be discovered, Tamar witnesses a full-grown Shelah and her father-in-law, Judah, on their way to Timnah. Not recognizing Tamar, Judah mistakes her for a prostitute and propositions her. Tamar accepts his offer upon the receipt of his signet, cord, and staff, which serve as a pledge that he will send a young goat to her as payment (vv 15–19). Unbeknownst to Judah, Tamar conceives a child by her father-in-law, which is a problem because she is an unwed widow. Upon hearing of Tamar's condition, and still unaware she carries his offspring, Judah demands that Tamar be burned to death. Tamar is able to thwart his fury (and her death), however, by proving that Judah is the father of the child she carries (vv 24–26).

The narrative concludes with Tamar's unconventional union with Judah, which results in the birth of twin sons to carry on the

---

6. Matthews and Benjamin, *Social World of Ancient Israel,* 23.
7. Ibid.

line. Tamar emerges as the heroine of the story. She takes great risks to further the plan of God, in spite of Judah's efforts to the contrary.

In Tamar's story, we see a woman from outside Israel who rises to prominence in Israel's historical record for rejecting the social constraints to which she was bound.

Rahab

If Tamar's radical heroism and rise to prominence is shocking, perhaps Rahab's is even more so. Rahab is named not only in the genealogy of Jesus but also remembered as one of the faithful in the "Annals of Faith" found in Hebrews 11 and in James 2:25–26. Rahab's story moves us forward several generations in the covenantal narrative, after the Exodus from Egypt as the Hebrew people prepare to enter the Promised Land. It is important to read Rahab's story in the context of the Joshua narrative and the larger metanarrative of Scripture in order to understand her role in the covenantal relationship and missional paradigm of Yahweh's activity in and through the people of Israel.

The narrative section that includes Rahab comes after the long wanderings in the wilderness; the death of Moses, Miriam, and Aaron; and the new generation of Israel who will find rest in the Promised Land (Josh 1). Joshua sends spies to scope out the land of Canaan, especially the city of Jericho. The spies "go into" the home of a woman named Rahab (Josh 2:1). In the Hebrew here, Rahab is described as a הַזּוֹנָה (harlot), the same word used to describe Tamar. Here too, the harlot emerges as the heroine: Rahab hides the spies from the messengers of Jericho's king (vv 2–4). Once the king closes the gates to prevent the intruders' escape, Rahab lowers the men down the wall and instructs them to hide in the hills until the king's men stop searching for them (vv 5–15). Before she lowers the men to safety, we find a crucial exchange between Rahab and the men of Israel. Rahab, who identifies herself as a Canannite, proclaims her knowledge of the one God of Israel who brought the people of Israel through the Sea of Reeds and rescued them from Egypt. The narrator tells us the men's hearts are "melted" by her faith and her

23

assurance that their God would take the city. So impressed are they by Rahab's faith that they ensure her safety and the safety of her family when the people of Israel attack the city, if she and her family remain inside the home marked by a scarlet cord.

John Stek points out that Rahab uses the "first person plural four times" to identify herself as a person of Canaan; thus, "when she speaks we hear the voice of a Canaanite."[8] Stek argues that Rahab's confession is both personal and communal—she speaks both of her individual belief and the fear and dread of the Canaanites before Yahweh, the God of Israel.[9] Further, Stek illustrates that Rahab's words follow the song of Moses found in Exodus 15:14–15:

> The nations will hear and tremble,
> Anguish will grip the people of Philistia;
> > The inhabitants of Canaan will quake
> Dread and terror will fall on them.[10]

With Stek's help, we see Rahab as a representative of the Canaanites, one who acknowledges the sovereignty of Israel's God instead of seeking to thwart Yahweh's promises to the children of Israel. *If only,* seems to be the implication, *the Canaanites were all like Rahab, all this destruction would not be necessary.*

As we note the function of Rahab's celebrated role in the narrative, we must also observe the paradox her presence brings to the story of Israel. According to the narrator, Yahweh has previously instructed the Israelites to take the land of Canaan, to spare no one and to make "no covenants" or treaties with the people (Ex 34:12–16; Deut 7:1–5; 23:6). Is this not exactly what the Israelite spies have done in their arrangement with Rahab?

> Joshua said to the two men who had spied out the land, "Go into the prostitute's house, and bring the woman out of it and all who belong to her, as you swore to her." So the young men

---

8. Stek, "Rahab of Canaan and Israel," 39.
9. Ibid., 40.
10. Ibid.

who had been spies went in and brought Rahab out, along with her father, her mother, her brothers, and all who belonged to her—they brought all her kindred out—and set them outside the camp of Israel. They burned down the city, and everything in it; only the silver and gold, and the vessels of bronze and iron, they put into the treasury of the house of the Lord. But Rahab the prostitute, with her family and all who belonged to her, Joshua spared. Her family has lived in Israel ever since. For she hid the messengers whom Joshua sent to spy out Jericho. (Josh 6:22–25 NRSV)

Yahweh's clear instructions are in tension with Rahab's courage. Rahab is a helper to Israel, and the messengers whom she helps are thus faithful to their promise to spare her and her family. Not only is Rahab spared, but she also becomes such a part of Israel that her legacy carries forth in the oral and written tradition well into the first centuries of the early church.

In the story of Rahab, we see once again a female character triumph over the limitations of her social status to participate in the plan of God for the future of Israel.

Ruth

Ruth stands as the ultimate contradiction to the perceived obscurity of women in the Old Testament. She is the ultimate feminine heroine: loyal, self-sacrificing, beautiful, and cunning. Although her story is too often reduced to a narrative vehicle that merely serves the genealogy of King David, her narrative starkly counters the male-dominated arc of Israel's story and is embroidered with deep theological meaning.

At issue in the Book of Ruth is *rest*. While Joshua and the Israelites seek rest in the Promised Land—rest that would be known only at the defeat of their enemies and possession of the land to which they held claim—for Ruth, for any woman, rest means a husband and male children. In the ancient world, the only protection a woman could hope for was ensured either by her father or her husband. Her prime import was the furtherance of the familial line through the bearing of children; a woman without father, husband, or son was without any power, protection, or provision in that society.

Women such as Ruth and Naomi were liminal, meaning they were without household.[11] In ancient Israel, the household was the basic social unit, the only domain shared by male and female.[12] The household functioned as the locus for all religious, economic, and political activities and was critical to the stability of the larger society. In an ancient agrarian society such as Israel, the household was a work space, an eating space, and a lodging space for a family, their animals, and whatever foreign travelers or guests the family welcomed.[13] Scripturally we find reference to the "house of my father" or occasionally "house of my mother," and these consist of a large extended family: parents, their sons, the wives and children of those sons, and unmarried daughters.[14]

In ancient Israel, "the orphan יתום, the prostitute הזנ, and the widow without children הגמלא" were all considered liminal; they were legally homeless and without any socioeconomic or political status.[15] It is precisely for women such as these that Yahweh makes provision and instructs the people of Yahweh to do likewise throughout the Old Testament. The provision and ethic of Yahweh is illustrated nowhere more beautifully than in the narrative of Ruth.

Ruth's story opens without specific date but instead with a vague assignment of time—literally, in the Hebrew, "in the days of judging of the judges" (1:1). Famine had driven Elimelech and Naomi from Bethlehem to Moab, where their two sons had married Moabite women. Elimelech and the sons died, leaving Naomi with her two daughters-in-law, Orpah and Ruth (vv 1–6). Naomi decides to return to Bethlehem of Judah, and so pleads with her daughters-in-law to return to their mothers' homes, knowing she

---

11. Matthews and Benjamin, *Social World of Ancient Israel*, 133.

12. Myers, "In the Household and Beyond," 21.

13. Ibid.

14. Ibid.

15. Matthews and Benjamin, *Social World of Ancient Israel*, 133.

is too old to provide sons whom they can later marry. Naomi instructs them to return to their families so they may find a חהונמ (resting place, v 9). Orpah agrees, after some objection, but Ruth confesses her allegiance to Naomi and vows to remain with her wherever she goes. The two return to Bethlehem (vv 10–18).

The Levitical provisions of Yahweh take effect when Ruth is able to glean from the field of a wealthy landowner, Boaz, who is a relative of Naomi's (2:1–6; see also Lev 19:9; 23:33; Deut 24:19). Boaz is a Hebrew who is faithful to the admonitions of Yahweh; he happily allows Ruth to glean and encourages her to remain in his fields, where she will not be harmed. Further, he is impressed with her loyalty to Naomi and assures Ruth she will find safety under the כנכ (wing) of Yahweh (2:7–12). Shortly thereafter, Ruth asks Boaz to spread his כנכ (wing) over her, such that Boaz serves as an extension of Yahweh's provision by attempting to proceed with the Levirate marriage rites (3:1ff).

Although the specifics of the Levirate don't exactly fit Ruth's situation, it is clear the narrator wants us to understand Ruth and Boaz's marriage in these terms. A debate about the marriage is taken up at the city gate between Boaz and the nearer kinsman, who waives his right to Ruth and Elimelech's inheritance (4:1–10). Here Boaz raises the names of Elimelech's dead sons and vows to continue the family line, which, according to Davies and others, is the first purpose of the Levirate arrangement.[16]

Ruth emerges as yet another female heroine from outside the Hebrew family who continues the line of Israel from Abraham to David. Ruth and Boaz's son, Obed, becomes father to Jesse, father to David (4:17). Ruth is described by the narrator as "better than seven sons" because her loyalty and obedience save the family line (4:15).

Bathsheba

Each of these women has some sort of scandal attached to her story—Tamar poses as a prostitute, Rahab is a harlot of Jericho, Ruth

---

16. Davies, "Inheritance Rights," 140.

seeks out Boaz at the threshing floor—and Bathsheba is no exception. Up to this point in the grand narrative, each woman has been an outsider (though we are never made certain of Tamar's family of origin, Canaanite seems likely); each has found herself powerless in the socioeconomic and political structure of ancient Israel; and each has emerged from scandal to find redemption through Yahweh's deliverance. Bathsheba, wife of Uriah the Hittite, follows this same literary model.

David is made king over all Israel following the deaths of Saul, Jonathan, and Ishbosheth (2 Sam 1–5). In covenant with Yahweh, David brings the Ark of God to Jerusalem, where he establishes his capitol, pushing back the Philistines, defeating the Ammonites and Arameneans—and then taking a fall from his rooftop. David sees Bathsheba bathing and thinks she is beautiful. But he doesn't stop there. Upon learning she is Uriah's wife, David sends for Bathsheba anyway and sleeps with her (2 Sam 11:1–4). Let's be clear: no blame should be ascribed to Bathsheba. Any objection to the king's bidding would mean certain death. Recalling Bathsheba as some "bad girl of the Bible" is a failure to recognize the nature of an ancient society under the rule of a monarchy. All responsibility here lies at the feet of the king, God's man David, who not only fathers a child with another man's wife but has her husband killed to cover up his transgression (2 Sam 11:5–26).

Upon Uriah's death, Bathsheba becomes one of David's many wives and bears the child they conceived together, only to lose him to death as an infant (2 Sam 12). David later confesses his sin and mourns their child, and eventually he and Bathsheba conceive another son, Solomon. Although Solomon is not David's son in direct line to succeed him as king, Bathsheba's son will inherit the crown (1 Kings 1). It is Bathsheba herself, with the help of the prophet Nathan, who accomplishes Solomon's ascension to David's throne. She understands the risk to her son if any other becomes king; it was common practice for new kings to execute their brothers to eliminate possible rivals. Robert I. Vasholz suggests that, by exposing the treachery of David's heir, Adonijah, Bathsheba all but forces

David to acknowledge Solomon instead. Vasholz writes, "Here was a very wise woman (and mother) whose acumen not only helped her son to secure his reign, but who also demonstrates wisdom as a virtue of God's kingdom." [17]

In Bathsheba, we see more than a beautiful victim of David's crimes; we see a woman devoted to the preservation of the Davidic kingdom through her son and rightful heir, Solomon. She stands in league with her sisters Tamar, Rahab, and Ruth, who rose above the circumstances of their culture and birth to further the work of God on earth. These women and their actions were unorthodox, unlikely, even unceremonious, yet it is these very women who were recorded in the ancient annals of Israel and who became foremothers to the Messiah.

Conclusion

In the lives of the Old Testament women found in the genealogy of Christ, God's activity in and through the lives of women could not be more obvious. In a history devoted primarily to the patriarchal narrative and the formation of the monarchy, these women hold prominent places. Their lineage will usher in the Messiah. Tracing their remarkable stories, we are able to conclude that God is not reluctant to transcend the limitations and constraints of human society, often choosing women—powerless and without status or social capital—as conduits through whom to work. In the narrative history of Israel, the faith, fidelity, and righteousness of women is sometimes demonstrated over and against their male counterparts, as in the cases of Tamar and Bathsheba. In other instances, as in the stories of Rahab and Ruth, men recognize the God-ordained roles women must play and then willingly partner with them in the work of God.

The voices of these women ring to us across the ages, as we study the sacred texts of our faith. Their stories remind us once again that God has always called women and empowered them to serve God's people—and ever shall.

---

17. Vasholz, "Wisdom of Bathsheba," 49.

About the Author

Kimberly Majeski is a scholar, preacher, and author who challenges her audiences to find the life-transforming connection between their personal story and the inspiring ancient story of the Scriptures. A native of Nashville, Tennessee, Kimberly brings a dose of Southern charm to her scholarship. As a radio personality, conference speaker, women's retreat leader, Bible teacher, and pastor, Kimberly captivates audiences with her ability to exposit biblical truths through storytelling that is engaging, transparent, and uplifting.

Kimberly has served in many pastoral and leadership roles in local and national contexts, including campus pastor of Anderson University and ministry coordinator of Women of the Church of God. Today Kimberly writes a popular weekly blog that can be found at www.kimberlymajeski.com and is the founder of Butterflies of Hope Outreach, a ministry to exotic dancers in her city.

Kimberly is an ordained minister of the Church of God and has completed postgraduate education at the University of Notre Dame and Anderson University School of Theology, where she obtained her doctoral degree in 2009. Kimberly currently serves as the assistant professor of biblical studies at Anderson University School of Theology and as a co-host for the Christians Broadcasting Hope radio program *ViewPoint*. Kimberly and her husband Kevin reside in Anderson, Indiana, with their two black cats, Monkey and Henry.

CHAPTER 3

Biblical Precedents for Women in Ministry

BY SHARON PEARSON

The Church of God (Anderson, Indiana) historically has held a high view of Scripture. The Bible is recognized as the authority for faith and life in the church. For a church that claims the integrity and authority of Scripture, questions of practice are taken seriously. An early motto, "The Bible is our creed," is a classic expression of that conviction. This motto assumes it is possible to be directed by Scripture. The Church of God refused any attempt to define the revelation contained in Scripture in any "man-made creed." This refusal is one of high principle and a certain wisdom, yet is a source of anxiety for many in the church, for in it are the seeds of diversity. We may not all agree on exactly what the Bible says about a particular situation. Yet most in the church (at least those who are thoughtful) are willing to live within the tension of a unity born only of the fellowship of salvation in order not to place our perspectives above what is in Scripture.

On the issue of women in church leadership, there is, as with so many other issues, tension in Scripture. Peter's first sermon, explaining and defending events of the day of Pentecost (Acts 2)—including the prophesying of women—is based on the eschatological (end-times) prophecy of the book of Joel. In other books of the New Testament, there are other types of teachings about women, statements that seem to be based on pragmatic concerns and social convention. Appeals to a hierarchical order and a dominance-subordination paradigm in the Pastoral Epistles stand alongside stories of the revolutionary attitudes and practice of Jesus' ministry and in Paul's references to the participation of women in the ministry of the early church. When there is disparity between the biblical presentations, Christians must carefully observe and explain that disparity if we are to have integrity in our interpretation and application of Scripture.

Especially where the church places high value on Scripture, it is important to talk about biblical precedents when discussing questions not explicitly answered in Scripture. When we explore Scripture to determine whether, and how, women were involved in ministry in the early church, we must be careful. Some in today's church have said that women should not be allowed to even speak up in a service of worship, much less lead a congregation. Others have said a woman may function in a pastoral role, but only if she is under the authority of a man. Still other church communities have long recognized women in full ministerial and leadership roles and positions in the church.

All serious (and even not-so-serious) Bible students interpret Scripture according to some set of principles. They may not be aware of their principles or of how and where they apply their presuppositions, yet when anyone looks to Scripture to answer a question, they make choices about which texts should be considered, which text is of greater value, and how various texts should be evaluated together to answer their particular question. Then the student must ask how their interpretation applies to the church's situation today. How does the church act on what is learned in the study of Scripture?

All decide which texts of Scripture are timeless and always directly applicable, and which texts are a cultural expression of a principle in a particular setting. If you doubt this statement, do you have a portion of Scripture posted on the door of your house? Do you give away all you have to feed the poor? Do you have a tattoo? Do you believe a father is allowed to put his children to death? All of these practices are addressed in Scripture. Although many have read the apostle Paul's instructions about women and wearing a veil for public worship, very few church groups actually require such a practice today. That instruction has been identified as a culturally bound instruction addressed to people in a particular time and circumstance.

Even where we conclude that particular instructions do not apply to modern church practice, it is still important to determine the concern or the principle behind the instructions. What principle lies behind this or that teaching of Paul's? The issue then, for students of the Bible, is not whether to make such distinctions but where to draw the line in that process. In fact, such issues arise exactly because of the nature of many of the texts in the New Testament: They are letters addressed to particular churches in various locations in the ancient Mediterranean world. The writers are often addressing real problems or disputes between Christians (sometimes even church leaders) in particular locations. For an example, see Galatians 2:11, where Paul reports that he confronted Peter "to his face" and argues against other leaders who require that Gentiles be circumcised in order to be Christians.

In my own choices about how I select and evaluate and interpret texts of Scripture, I am governed by two almost automatic instincts. First, I believe that we are allowed to define an expression as limited to a particular circumstance (with a corresponding application) when we have a clear statement about the limits within that text or a differing position in other texts. For example, most Christians do not sell all they have to give to the poor, as Jesus instructed the rich young ruler (Luke 18:18–3). Most do not practice the Christian "socialism" of the early church in Jerusalem; they do not give all their personal goods to the apostles to be distributed so that no believer is "in need" (Acts 2:43–47; 4:32–37). That practice was understood to be fulfillment of the laws of Deuteronomy 15 and Leviticus 25. Many Christians look at other texts that are understood to allow for private ownership. They appeal to the fact that Jesus defines the disreputable Zacchaeus as "saved" even though he gives only half of everything away. He also pays back what he, in effect, has stolen by four times over, fulfilling the law of Exodus 22:1 (Luke 19:1–10).

The second primary principle I apply in interpreting Scripture is an old dictum: "Where the text speaks, I speak." But where Scripture is silent or unclear, I speak only with a great deal of humility. A big problem is that some of the questions we address to Scripture are foreign to it and may be worked out only by implication. The question this chapter addresses, that of women in church leadership, is not foreign to the New Testament but is not answered explicitly, and some of the implications are not immediately clear. What *is* clear is that women did participate in the ministry of the early church. But there are no texts that clearly define women's participation in ministry according to office and authority. Therefore, all who address this question to the New Testament are working by implication, even when they do not recognize that they are doing so.

To answer the question, "Should women be recognized as ministers in the church and hold positions of authority?" it is necessary to review information on women in general in the New Testament. What we should remember at the outset of our investigation is that stories about Jesus and the early church were selected and put into "books" of various forms (e.g., gospels, epistles) and these books, recognized as authoritative, were collected over a long period of time into what we now know as the Holy Bible (the word *Bible* means "books"). It is amazing that stories about women, their personal names, and their participation in the church survived.

Why? Because such material was preserved in an androcentric (man-centered) society. The cultures out of which the Bible comes were patriarchal (ruled by males) and patrilineal (property and name passed through male lineage) societies in which women were counted as property, and were referred to by their father's or their husband's names. So, it is remarkable that women were included in the story at all. There is an abundance of evidence, however, in the various accounts of women in the New Testament that shows that women were an integral part of the life of the church and that the gospel could not be told without including these individuals.

Women in the Gospels

It is impossible to consider the place of women in the church without recalling Jesus' attitude and actions toward the women around him. Women, as well as men, were compelled to follow Jesus during his short years of ministry. A number of women traveled with Jesus' ragged band of followers, even though to allow such was unthinkable in that culture. Jeremias calls this reality "an unprecedented happening in history of that time."[1] We know about these women from short references in the Gospels that many persons reading Scripture miss, especially in their import (Mark 15:40–41; Luke 8:1–3). These references indicate that a group of women supported Jesus and his disciples financially. They were women with means, probably from an upper echelon of society. The Mark account paints a poignant picture of these women at the scene of Jesus' crucifixion. The three women named in that account visit Jesus' burial site after Sabbath to anoint their Lord's body for burial. And then, in a society where a woman's testimony was not allowed in court, they were commissioned by Jesus to be the first to proclaim his resurrection (Mark 16:1–8). Nothing was more natural than their being among the 120 who waited in the upper room for the power that would give fire to their lives and witness. The church, from its inception, included women.

---

1. Jeremias, *Jerusalem in the Time of Jesus*, 374

Who were the women who sought out Jesus and became a part of the gospel story? They were the three who became known as leaders among the group of women: Mary Magdalene, Mary the mother of Joses, and Salome. They were Mary and Martha who, contrary to social rules, invited Jesus into their home. They included the woman unclean with a feminine infirmity and the Samaritan woman at the well. They were the Syrophonecian (Gentile) woman who asked him for "the crumbs" for her demon-possessed daughter and the woman who anointed his feet. The significance of the stories about women in the Gospels is that they were recorded and preserved at all. In a culture where women were property and had no rights or privileges, these stories themselves would have laid open the early church to criticism and contempt. Furthermore, in every story about Jesus with women, the import, which most Bible readers miss, is that Jesus crossed all lines of propriety, both religious and social. His very actions were a challenge to the cherished traditions of his own people. He went so far as to commend women as examples of faith and spiritual vitality, women who were not counted in the number of a synagogue and who were sequestered behind a screen, separated from men in their acts of worship. At the religious center of their world, the temple in Jerusalem, women were restricted to an outer court. A husband could overturn his wife's religious vow to God. And yet Jesus lifted them up as models of religious piety and examples of faith (e.g., the woman who gave her small coins, Luke 21:1–4), and appeared first to them after his resurrection.

The story of Mary and Martha has special significance. In this story, Mary sits at Jesus' feet. Those of us who do not know the history and culture of the Jews miss the fact that disciples (followers) sat at the feet of their rabbis (religious teachers). A rabbi taught only boys and men. But here, Jesus, as the Teacher, instructs Mary in the same way he taught the men who followed him. To the rabbis, this was an unheard of breach of ethics, religious custom, and social decorum. Some rabbis of that time period said things like "Better to burn the Torah than to teach it to a woman" and

"He who teaches his daughter the law, teaches her lechery."[2] As if teaching Mary were not enough, Jesus is recorded as even chiding Martha for fulfilling her socially prescribed role instead of joining Mary (Luke 10:38–42).

The cumulative effect of these stories is compelling evidence that Jesus broke custom by championing women as equally worthy as men of his concern and ministry. His evaluation of them far outstripped the most expansive and tolerant in his day and continually surprised even those who knew him well. The tone of his ministry was not to accept the status quo, but rather to model a new life and relationships for women. The popular attitude of the day was that women were responsible for all sexual temptation and, therefore, sexual sin. Yet Jesus challenged the sexist standards of his world: the lustful glance of a man (Matt 5:27–32), the casual divorce—a male prerogative (Matt 19:3–9), and the threat of capital punishment applied unfairly only to the adulterous woman (John 8:1–11).[3] None of the stories about Jesus with women would be approved, much less applauded, outside of the early church that preserved them. Yet such events were so integral to the reality of the Jesus community that they make up a significant part of the gospel.

An anticipated defense against this evidence in consideration of the question of women in ministry is that none of the women following Jesus became one of the twelve disciples. None of the twelve apostles were women. None were accorded equality. It is not necessary to argue the cultural barriers here. It is enough to respond that no Gentiles were allowed such a privilege either, yet this fact does not prohibit non-Jews from the leadership and offices of the church today.

Women in the Early Church
Women were an integral part of the Jesus community that awaited the empowerment of the Spirit (Acts 1:14–17), and women were among those who received the Spirit in fulfillment of Joel's

---

2. Ibid., 373.
3. Ibid., 370.

prophecy (Acts 2:1-4). In the same way that it is incredible that stories of women were incorporated into the Gospel accounts, it is also a wonder that participation of women in the early church was recorded in Acts and the Epistles. Against all cultural expediency and propriety, their stories are told in Scripture. A brief perusal of the evidence of their participation can be listed in two categories: (1) lists of women with particular titles or descriptors of function, and (2) references to women's participation in ministry.

1. Lists of Women

One type of evidence in the New Testament is the brief, often incidental, reference to women in various texts of the New Testament. These women are identified as participating in various aspects of the ministry of the church. First, these women are referred to by their own personal names, a fact that is countercultural and would not have been applauded in the general culture.

The apostle Paul refers to numerous women by name. Priscilla, listed in several epistles in the New Testament, evidently bore quite a reputation (Acts 18:2, 18, 26; 1 Cor 16:19; Rom 16:3-4; 2 Tim 4:19). How many other leaders were referred to as often, or in such a variety of texts? Priscilla, along with Aquila, taught Apollos (Acts 18:26). Against rabbinic tradition that identified women only as "the wife" of the man who is named, the apostle Paul recognized Priscilla by name as prominent enough to be listed along with her husband. Even more, he put her name *first* in the pair more often than not (four of six times). Also, by calling Priscilla a "fellow worker" in Christ Jesus, the apostle Paul accorded to Priscilla (as well as Aquila) an equal place among such other workers as Timothy (Rom 16:21), Titus (2 Cor 8:23), Luke (Philem 24), Apollos, and Paul (1 Cor 3:9).

One reference applied to Priscilla, "fellow worker," is also applied to Euodia and Syntyche, leaders at Philippi. Paul uses the same descriptors of Euodia and Syntyche that he applies to Timothy and Epaphroditus (Phil 2:25; 4:2-3). He claims that Euodia and

Syntyche contended with him "in the gospel" or "in the work of the gospel," just as Timothy had (Phil 2:22).

Phoebe is called a *prostatis* (overseer, guardian; Rom 16:1–2), the term used to indicate elders who "preside" (1 Tim 5:17), "rule" (Rom 12:8), or "hold authority over" (1 Thess 5:12). Phoebe is also called a "minister." In the KJV, the Greek term, elsewhere always translated as "minister," is translated as "servant" only in Phoebe's case. The title applied to the leaders Apollos (1 Cor 3:5), Timothy (1 Tim 4:6), and Paul (1 Cor 3:5) is also applied to Phoebe. "The Seven" of Acts 6:1–6 are traditionally recognized as the first of such "deacons" (Phil 1:11; Tim 3:8–13). Of the seven, Stephen teaches and corrects like a presbyter or bishop (Acts 6:9–10; cf. 20:17, 28), and Philip is called an "evangelist."

Four women are listed in the closing instructions of Paul's letter to the Romans as having "worked very hard" in the Lord: Mary, Tryophena, Tryphosa, and Persis. The apostle Paul applied that same description to the ministries of other male leaders in the church (1 Cor 16:15–16; 1 Thess 5:12; 1 Tim 5:17).

Finally, it is probable that the reference in Romans 16:7 to two who were "outstanding among the apostles" included a woman. The person in question is referred to as "Junias" in the KJV. But this cannot be correct. That would be like identifying "Sue" as a man. David Scholer's review of the evidence is most helpful:

> Junias is a male name in English translations, but there is no evidence that such a male name existed in the first century A.D. Junia, a female name, was common, however. The Greek grammar of the sentence…means that the male and female forms of this name would be spelled identically…Since Junia is the name attested in the first century and since the great church father…of the fourth century, John Chystostom (no friend of women in history), understood the reference to be to a woman Junia, we ought to see it that way as well. In fact, it was not until the thirteenth century that she was changed to Junias.[4]

---

4. Scholer, "Women in Ministry," 12-13.

Then there are texts that do not name women. In Acts 21, Philip the evangelist (one of "the Seven" of Acts 6) is noted for the gift given to his four daughters, the gift of prophecy (to prophesy was the gift the apostle Paul thought of as the most important gift, 1 Cor 14:1). We are not told how these prophets expressed their gift in their community. This information affirms Peter's quotation of Joel's prophecy in his sermon on the day of Pentecost. God declares through Joel: "Your daughters shall prophesy...even upon... women...I will pour out my Spirit; and they shall prophesy" (Acts 2:17–18 NRSV).

It is obvious from these informal, uncontrived lists that women played a significant role as leaders in the early church. Their function in ministry is defined in those places by the same terms applied to the ministry of men, without distinction in role or function. It is also clear that both the actual ministry and the record of that ministry were more limited for women than for men.

2. Evidence of Participation: 1 Corinthians

If we knew the world of Jesus and Paul, we would remember that women did not participate in services at the synagogue. They were in a separate area and often behind a screen. It is remarkable then that women participated in Christian worship services, which first followed synagogue practices. The earliest Christians were Jews who attended local synagogue services on the Sabbath and special events at the temple in Jerusalem.

One of the strongest pieces of evidence for women's participation in the worshiping community comes from a brief argument in one of Paul's early epistles. First Corinthians 11:2-16 makes explicit reference to women prophesying and praying in services of worship. Paul is not commenting on the fact of women praying or prophesying in worship; he is only concerned about *in what way* they are doing such. Their participation in services of worship is evidently assumed under the wide rubric of spiritual gifts and ministries that have been designated to all, regardless of religious, social, or sexual distinctions, for "the common good" (1 Cor 12:7).

First Corinthians 11:3 is one of the basic assertions often appealed to in the discussion of women in ministry: "Now, I want you to realize that the head of every man is Christ, and the head of the woman is man, and the head of Christ is God." While it seems obvious that the apostle Paul is appealing to some sort of order here, the meaning and application of the statement is much less clear. This statement is made in service of Paul's argument that women should not abandon head-covering in their exercise of ministry (public prayer and prophecy). Whatever this statement does mean, it in no way functions in this text to limit the participation or leadership of women in public worship. It is meant rather to maintain the "natural" tradition of head-covering.

The term *head* is most often translated elsewhere in the Bible (and other literature of the time) as "origin" or "source." Translation of *head* in these terms means something quite different than when understood as "chief" or "master" or "lord." If translated as "lord," women could use this passage to promote the idolatry of men. Women would owe men what men owe Christ! While Paul *is* appealing to the order of creation from Genesis 2:18–23, he does not go so far as a straight parallel would allow. He does not claim that woman is the *image* as well as glory of man (1 Cor 11:7). Woman, too, shares the image of God and therefore is not more removed from God than man; Paul concedes this to Genesis 1:27 and 5:2.[5]

Verse 8 restates the concept of origin or source in the order of creation. It may be that priority includes a sense of superiority here, but that meaning is not supported by the text in Genesis.[6] Paul makes a summary statement in verse 10: "For this reason and because of the angels, the woman ought to have a sign of authority on her head" (NIV 1984). The common translation of this text is misleading. The Greek term for *authority* should be translated just as it is in the Greek text: that woman should have "authority" on her head. Translators have added references to a "sign" of authority or the "veil" in an attempt to make sense of the text and the context.[7]

---

5. Barrett, *First Epistle to the Corinthians*, 248–49.

6. See discussion below, "Argument from Creation Accounts."

7. Scholer, "Women in Ministry," 17.

The angels Paul appeals to in his argument (11:10) are understood to be guardians of the created order who would be offended by oversight of the principle of sexual differentiation. In this case, the head-covering now not only symbolizes woman's glorification of man but also her authority to play an active role in worship. As Barrett argues, "That is, her veil represents the new authority given to women under the new dispensation to do things which formerly had not been permitted."[8] This interpretation is supported by the two verses which follow. Having argued for natural differences between man and woman, Paul now lays down a new principle of mutuality and interdependence based also on the order of creation (1 Cor 7:3–4).

Three chapters after the incidental reference to women praying and prophesying in worship, come words from Paul that are appealed to often to repress women in church: "Women should be silent in the churches. For they are not permitted to speak" (1 Cor 14:26–40). These words confront us. They seem to limit the role of women in worship, even though women have already been recognized as participating and even leading in worship. The apparent discontinuity between these two passages has been explained in a variety of ways.[9] But no matter what final conclusion you take from these words, it cannot be that women are not allowed to participate in public worship. Ralph Martin summarizes some options and then places the evidence in the larger context of Paul's work and writings:

> Paul remains committed to social egalitarianism in the gospel (Gal. 3:28), and there is the undeniable evidence of the role he accorded women colleagues (Phoebe, Prisca [Priscilla], the women of Philippi [Phil. 4:3, sic.] and the several coworkers in Rom. 16). It is prima facie unlikely he should state categorically "Let your women keep silent" in worship.[10]

---

8. Barrett, *First Epistle to the Corinthians*, 255.
9. Martin, *Spirit and the Congregation*, 84–88.
10. Ibid., 85.

The best solution, one that gives fair consideration to all of the evidence, is to attend both to the context of Paul's statement and also the verb translated "speak" (Greek *lalein*). In Paul's correction of disorder in the services and of persons who are claiming to be prophets with "special powers" (14:37), he silences three groups. Women are the third group identified. If one recognizes the use of the verb *lalein* to mean "inspired speech" (or their understanding of tongues-speaking), then the picture drawn by the text and the larger context of this epistle is that such women aspired to be charismatic teachers. They are claiming special revelations in inspired speech (tongues) that they consider to be above the usual corrections of the congregation and apostolic teaching. Their claims are so inflated that the apostle resorts to sarcasm: "Did the word of God originate with you? Or are you the only people it has reached?"(v 36 NIV).

The letter to the Corinthians addresses a number of errors and misunderstandings of the faith. Gross competition and heretical teaching are going on in the Corinthian church. Some of the heretical teaching can be identified as an incipient gnosticism (that later developed into full-blown Gnosticism). These women, claiming special knowledge, may have been responsible for the speculation that there was no actual resurrection of the body but that a spiritual resurrection occurred at baptism. These speculations prompted Paul's extended reply that begins with his question, "How can some of you say that there is no resurrection of the dead?" (15:12 NIV). Their denial of the resurrection lay in the claim that Christians were raised at baptism—they were angelic beings (13:1), a misapplication of Jesus' words, such as those found in Luke 20:35–36. This misinterpretation had led to confusion in the home: As resurrected beings, they no longer participated in marriage obligations; they were attempting to live in a state of celibacy in marriage (1 Cor 7:3–5).

Such heretical teachers (women *glossolalics*, tongues speakers) were to be kept "under control" as the "law" required (*nomos*, meaning "principle," and here referring to Paul's teaching; see v 37).

The meaning of "asking their husbands at home" is a response to the challenge these women presented to their husbands in public assembly. The verb "inquire after" (*eperotan,* v 35) is used in the sense of interrogation, in the same way as they were challenging apostolic authority. This interpretation fits the larger portrait drawn of the women in the Corinthian church. These women were abusive of their new-found freedoms in the church. They discarded their head-covering (11:5) and practiced a negative spirituality full of pride and competition. This portrait, drawn carefully by Martin, is supported by a parallel circumstance found in 1 Timothy 2:8–15, in which arrogant women have aspired to be teachers of things about which they do not know (possibly also teaching gnostic perspectives).[11]

Finally, it is helpful to remember that there was a temple devoted to Aphrodite, the goddess of love, on the Acrocorinth, 1,800 feet above the ancient city of Corinth. The women creating problems in the Corinthian church were women who had come from a culture steeped in goddess worship. For a man, engaging in sex with a priestess at the temple was considered a form of worship. (That is why Paul addresses some members of the church who were engaging with prostitutes [6:12–20].) Tongues-speaking was also practiced at Delphi, just across the bay from Corinth. Priestesses at the temple of Delphi inhaled natural gases from the earth and then spoke ecstatic oracles (tongues)—for a price. We should not be surprised that defining Christian worship, spiritual practices, and the place of women in the church in such contexts was so challenging.

The above discussions about the participation of women in public worship and lists of women who led in the early church offer evidence that women functioned in ministry leadership in the early church. While there is no claim to *office* here, there is no question but that the *function* of ministry and leadership occurred.

---

11. Ibid., 86–88.

The Use of Household Codes in the Epistles

One significant aspect of the argument against recognizing women as ministers in the church are texts in the New Testament that refer to household codes, or station codes, of the Graeco-Roman world. The New Testament authors did not create these household codes but quoted from the cultural authorities of that day.[12] The Greek philosopher Aristotle, who predated Christ by three and a half centuries, was the source of the formal arrangement of pairings based on the dominant–subordinate hierarchical model:

> The primary and smallest parts of the household are master and slave, husband and wife, father and children...Authority and subordination are conditions not only inevitable but also expedient...There is always found a ruling and a subject factor...between the sexes, the male is by nature superior and the female inferior, the male ruler and the female subject.[13]

Aristotle expanded this household code to the realm of political life because, in his thinking, "the household was a microcosm of the state."[14] He taught the authority/subordination model in the pairing of ruler/people. He promoted this social order as necessary to stability, harmony, and political security. The Roman Empire of the first century AD considered any threat to this Aristotelian value system a threat to stability and security. So the Roman emperor Octavian instructed his soldiers to "allow no woman to make herself equal to a man."[15] What was the occasion for such a concern? Likely Anthony and Cleopatra. David Balch reviews the problem as follows:

> If democratic equality between husband and wife as it existed in Egypt were allowed to influence Roman households, the government would degenerate into a democracy; and the

---

12. See Elliott, *Home for the Homeless;* Balch, *Wives Be Submissive,* 161–73.

13. Aristotle, *Politics* I, 1253b.

14. Balch, "Early Christian Criticism," 161–63.

15. Casius, *Roman History,* 50.25.3 and 28.3.

Romans believed this changed form of government would be morally worse than the aristocracy or monarchy which had brought them to power. The Egyptian Cleopatra's goddess Isis, who "gave women the same power as men" was perceived as a threat to continued Roman rule.[16]

The rights of the one in authority were assumed. Tyranny was considered merely an expression of that authority in the dominant culture, as we see in Aristotle's words: "For there is no such thing as injustice in the absolute sense towards what is one's own."[17] Women were owned by men, and whatever men had to do to protect and control their property was just and right.

This lengthy look back has been necessary so that we may recover the meaning of the household codes as they appear in the New Testament and as original audiences understood them. The significance of the household codes in the New Testament is not that they required submission; the whole culture already enforced that. Household codes were not simply *adopted* by New Testament authors; rather, the authors *adapted* them. The codes were qualified in significant ways in earlier New Testament texts (in chronological order, Col 3:18–41; Eph 5:21–6:9; 1 Peter 2:13–3:7). They were not accepted as absolutes; they were critiqued even as they were cited. For example, in Colossians 3:18–4:1, the traditional pairings are each followed by what, to a Graeco-Roman man, would be unthinkable modifications. The New Testament authors used the original codes to serve a higher purpose:

wives be subject to husbands—husbands love wives
children obey parents—fathers do not provoke children
slaves obey masters—masters treat slaves justly[18]

The original audience of the New Testament epistles, upon receiving the instructions on the left side of these pairings, would not

16. Balch, "Early Christian Criticism," 162–63.
17. Aristotle *Nicomachean Ethics*, V.1134b.
18. Balch, "Early Christian Criticism," 161.

have thought to challenge them. They would have recognized the familiar, the *status quo*. What they would have noticed immediately were the qualifications made to the code, the material on the right side of the pairings. Those given instruction on the right side are not the powerless of the community; the powerful are addressed. Such ethical requirements would doubtless have been cause for concern for the powers that be of the congregations and the powerful in the surrounding communities.

In Ephesians 5:21–23, we find reference to the household codes. In many versions of the Bible, the text is laid out as if verse 22 is the start of a new paragraph. This is misleading. In the original Greek text, verses 18–23 are one long sentence! (Paul is known for long sentences.) What we read as verse 18 begins with "be filled with the Spirit." What we read as verse 21 explains what being filled with the Spirit looks like: "Submit to one another out of reverence for Christ." What we read as verse 22 does not actually include the verb *submit*; it is inferred from the previous phrase. Paul writes: "Wives, do to your own husbands as you do to the Lord." Remember, all wives in that culture already knew such rules. What is unusual here is that they are being instructed to embed their obedience in their Spirit-filled lives, being submissive to one another as to the Lord—*not* because they are created to be inferior.

The ancient ear would have been most struck by the instruction that husbands, too, should submit to their wives (v 21). Further, Paul also asks husbands to love their wives as Christ loved the church by giving up his life for it. A husband is to give himself sacrificially for his wife (v 26). Paul gives this instruction to men who have married wives in a contract so as to produce legitimate heirs, and in a culture where men had concubines and visited prostitutes. Paul is not speaking of an emotional attachment. He envisions active giving of the self for the highest good of another. How differently this passage is read and preached today.

Likewise in Ephesians 5, the command to Christian masters is full of the seeds of change: "Treat your slaves in the same way" (that is, by the same set of attitudes and conduct required of Christian slaves). Such radical qualifications of the household codes are a class apart from any parallel in Greek philosophy, Stoicism, or Roman household codes.[19] And the seeds of such thinking assuredly produced such fruit as Paul's letter to Philemon, in which he requests that this slave master live a revolutionary change of relationship with his slave, Onesimus.

First Peter also sets conditions on the household codes. In the social setting of crisis, where Christians are being persecuted, submission to human authority (that is, the persecutors) is for the Lord's sake. Christians were suffering unjustly at the hands of tyrannical masters (2:19–20), husbands (3:6), and local government officials (2:14; 3:14–17). According to this epistle, Christians should adopt a practical strategy for survival when they are persecuted. The purpose for the appeal to the household code in 1 Peter is not to insist on conformity to traditional values. The purpose is to inspire Christian commitment even when it involves suffering at the hand of evildoers, and to challenge believers to trust the God who judges justly.[20] No question of female inferior nature comes up here. All believers are called to live as "servants of God" (2:16). Christ as the "suffering servant of God" is the model to follow (2:21–24).

In the instruction to slaves in 1 Peter, different terms for "slave" and "master" are used than in Colossians or Ephesians. In Paul's letters, the term used for servant in reference to household codes is *doulos* and for master, *kurios*. Here in 1 Peter, the terms used are *oiketai*, "household servants," and *despotai*, despots. The reason for these different terms is that the author has already used the term "servant" (*doulos*) to mean every Christian (2:16). The author has already used "master" (or *kurios*) to refer to God (2:15). While 1 Peter recognizes that Roman authorities might not judge justly as God has ordained they should (2:13–14) and as God does (2:21–23), the author still appeals to the code. Authorities are still to be submitted to—but notice the difference: "for the Lord's sake."

19. Balch, "Early Christian Criticism."

20. Martin, *Mark: Evangelist and Theologian.*

Likewise, Christian wives are to submit to pagan husbands, not because women are inferior, but for the purpose of evangelism (3:1–2). Furthermore, they are not to fear pagan husbands (3:6). And a Christian husband is called to a relationship with his wife that is distinctively different from the cultural norm. In fact, a most revolutionary concept appears here: The husband's spiritual vitality is actually dependent on the way he treats his wife.

The most significant critique of the household code in 1 Peter would be immediately obvious to the original hearers of that epistle. The Christian women addressed in 1 Peter 3 were married to pagan husbands. These women are assumed by the author to have freedom of religious choice. The norms of the Roman (and, in fact, Jewish) culture of that time did not allow such freedom. Plutarch expresses the typical Roman perspective:

> It is becoming for a wife to worship and know only the gods that her husband believes in, and to shut the door tight upon all queer rituals and outlandish superstitions. For with no god do stealthy and secret rites performed by a woman find any favor.[21]

Even while appealing to the social code of the day in this address to Christian wives, 1 Peter assumes their religious independence from their pagan husbands (cf. 1:18; 4:3–4). These women are encouraged to keep their faith and not to fear their husbands (who had likely expressed extreme displeasure and concern at their wives' conversions). When those women heard this epistle in a worship service, they heard a proclamation of freedom, religious responsibility, and increased value. Had their pagan husbands heard that same text, they would have heard insubordination and anarchy. And how would they have heard the words to their wives, "Do not give way to fear"? Without proper historical and cultural background, readers today all but miss the threat such teaching posed to the power structures of the day. If you believe Peter

---

21. Plutarch, *Advice to a Bride and Groom*, 140 D.

wrote this text, then you understand that the apostle had seen Jesus behave in revolutionary ways with women. Here he is asking the same of Christian husbands.

Many scholars have recognized the different way household codes are used in 1 Timothy and Titus. The predominant cultural attitudes of that day seem to have been adopted in the church by the time these epistles were written.[22] In these texts, there is no instruction to the dominant members of the hierarchy comparable to the leveling effect of the Colossians or Ephesians texts. And yet the motivation for requiring women and slaves to be subject is not based on the same assumptions as Aristotle or on the Roman belief in an inborn nature of inferior status. Rather, the instruction is to "be submissive" in order to avoid persecution, to win the acceptance of society, and "so that the Word of God may not be discredited" (Titus 2:5). These are pragmatic appeals, not unlike the exhortation to prayer in 1 Timothy 2:1–3. The purpose for both instructions is "that we may live peaceful and quiet lives" which will provide the opportunity for salvation of all.

First Timothy 2:11–15 is the text most often quoted by those who would limit the ministry of women. In fact, it has been used by some as the defining word of women's place in the church. "If there is one verse in the Bible more than any other which is used to disbar women from proclaiming the Good News of Jesus Christ and exercising their talents for his glory, it is 1 Timothy 2:12."[23] The passage is judged by some to be a clear statement of instruction for the church regarding women. Yet, the complexity and difficulty of the passage is mirrored in the very disagreement it engenders, even among conservative scholars. The text is a loose expression of the household codes. Yet even here in the most conservative expression of the code in the New Testament, the reason for submission is not grounded in the nature of creation, but rather in the story of the fall. The assertion of woman's greater culpability in the fall cannot be taken as a theological absolute. The Genesis account of

---

22. Jewett, *Man as Male and Female*, 149–59.

23. Kroeger and Kroeger, *I Suffer Not a Woman*, 12.

the fall (Gen 3) referred to in 1 Timothy 2:14 does not assign such a meaning to the woman succumbing first, before the man, to temptation. And the apostle Paul, when referring to the fall in his most complete doctrinal statement, talks about *Adam's* sin (Rom 5:12–14)—not Eve's. The claim that Adam was not the one deceived, that it was the woman who was deceived and became a sinner, cannot be equated with the Genesis or Romans references to this event. The claim is much more like the rabbinical speculations of that time as expressed, for example by Philo, the apostle Paul's older contemporary:

> ...the woman, being imperfect and deprived by nature, made the beginning of sinning; but man, as being the more excellent and perfect nature, was the first to set the example of blushing and being ashamed, and indeed of every good feeling and action.[24]

If 1 Timothy 2:12 ("I permit no woman to teach or have authority over a man; she is to keep silent" [NRSV]) is adopted as a propositional statement, as Paul's definitive (eternal and everywhere) word on restriction of the participation of women, then it follows that women must not participate in worship, must not be given leadership, and must be silent in services. However, once one begins literary and historical analysis, a number of serious challenges immediately arise. The first challenge is squaring how this text is undermined by other passages in which Paul promotes women's ministry. Another challenge has to do with the actual words used in the text. Interpretation of verse 12 depends on how one translates the verb *authentein* (infinitive, "to have authority"), which is a *hapax legomena* (a word that only occurs once) in the New Testament. The translator must rely on other nonbiblical sources to determine possible meanings. The term can mean four different things; each of these would radically affect the sense of the whole passage.[25]

---

24. Balch, *Wives Be Submissive*, 84.

25. The technical study of the use of this verb is meticulously presented in Kroeger and Kroeger, *I Suffer Not Woman*, 79-104.

The challenge posed by this passage is increased by the fact that two infinitives are placed back to back. A literal translation would read "to teach, to have authority." The infinitive verb *didaskein* (to teach) in 1 Timothy is always used in conjunction with another verb that qualifies its focus (see 1:3–4; 4:11; 6:2–3). Therefore, in verse 12, *authentein* is used to qualify the negative *content* of the teaching. It does not refer to the *activity* of teaching itself. Kroeger and Kroeger have concluded:

> If the context of 1 Timothy 2:12 is neutral and refers only to the activity of teaching rather than to its positive or negative content, then it is the only time that *didaskein* is so used in the Pastorals...it is in keeping with the other uses of *didaskein* to find in this directive a condemnation of their heterodoxy [false teaching].[26]

If it is an indirect statement with a repeated negative, the emphasis of the sentence is on the *content* of the teaching and not on the *function* of teaching.

In verse 2:12, the phrase "I do not permit" is better understood translated precisely from its grammatical form (a present continuous verb), as in "I am not permitting." Such an expression suggests specific instruction for a particular circumstance[27] and so would read with the implication "in this situation, I am not permitting."

Further difficulties are presented by the verses surrounding verse 12. In verse 11, the term used for "silence" is not the same as used in 1 Corinthians 14. The Greek term has five possible meanings, none of which is as strong as the term used in 1 Corinthians. The best translation here is "quietness" or "in a quiet demeanor"[28]— exactly the way it is translated just ten verses earlier (1 Tim 2:2). Here the same term exhorts prayers "so that we may lead a *quiet* and peaceable life" (cf. 2 Thess 3:12; 1 Thess 4:11). The term does

---

26. Kroeger and Kroeger, *I Suffer Not a Woman*, 81.
27. Fee, *1 & 2 Timothy, Titus*, 72.
28. Ibid.

not mean verbal silence per se, but an attitude of reverence or a state of peacefulness.

Another problem with 1 Timothy 2:8–15 is that Paul's usual term for a generic "man" is not used. In Pauline letters, *aner*, translated "man," occurs fifty times, and *gyne*, "woman," occurs fifty-four times (in eleven different texts). In each case, these terms refer to husbands and wives, not to a general male or female. The Pauline texts use *anthropos* when referring to a man or the male gender in general. So, is the submission required here of a generic woman to a generic man, or of a wife to a husband?

The relationship of verse 15 to the total passage is unclear; there is no consensus about the meaning of "she will be saved." Contextual and historical studies suggest that the passage is one of the several responses in the letter to false teachers at Ephesus. The content of that teaching may have included misunderstanding of the Old Testament, as well as imported ideas from the popular goddess religions, and may have been particularly attractive to women and to younger widows who avoided remarriage and had opened their homes to false teachers (2:9–15; 5:11–15; 2 Tim 3:6–7). Such teaching has been identified as a "precursor to Gnosticism" with "perversions of the Adam and Eve saga."[29] The later formal presentations of Gnosticism identified Eve as creator and as spiritual illuminator of Adam, and the serpent as offering "gnosis" to the world.[30] Adam was deceived into believing that he was created first.

All in all, the passage in 1 Timothy is best understood as part of the correction of false teachers and heretical teaching going on in at Ephesus, the location to which this letter is addressed (1:3).

---

29. Alan Padgett presents a compelling presentation for typology as the interpretive approach governing verses 11–15. Both Eve and the Ephesian women are deceived and "saved through childbirth," which recalls Genesis 3:15. Eve bears the seed that is at enmity with the serpent. Eve then is made both positive and negative type: "She is an example of deception in verses 13-14 and an example of salvation through childbirth in verse 15" (Padgett, "Wealthy Women at Ephesus").

30. Kroeger and Kroeger, in *I Suffer Not a Woman,* present a lengthy study of the cultural and historical influences behind the false teaching which include pagan goddess religions and Jewish mythologies and genealogies or origins as gnostic developments. They then read this passage, along with Padgett and others, as a refutation of false teaching (19–23, 62–66, 88–98, 103–77).

Ephesus was a center of pagan worship and goddess worship (Acts 19:23–41). The church there was in a life-and-death struggle with heresies that had a strong foothold in the congregation. First Timothy 2 insists that women learn correct doctrine and that the women involved in the heresies (including the false teaching that women must be in authority over men) not teach those heresies.

The false teaching at Ephesus may have been that it was a spiritual obstacle to bear children. In the context of Greek dualism, what was physical or material was evil; the goal of a spiritual being then was to rid oneself of the "flesh" and so to be more spiritual. Another perspective is that, given the high mortality rate of both mother and infant in birth, childbirth should be avoided or expectant mothers should appeal to a goddess for safety in childbearing. In light of the false teachings referred to variously in the Pastoral Epistles, the corrections of 1 Timothy 2 make sense. Women who had been lured by false teachings and were spreading them must be stopped.[31]

Considering the difficulties of interpreting 1 Timothy 2:11-15, it is remarkable—no, indefensible—that a single verse in the Bible, verse 12, is given such high status by some in the church. Even more, it is incredible that one single verse would be made the basis for any doctrine, especially when it runs counter to other evidence. Whatever one finally makes of this passage, if one counts the epistle as Pauline, one must consider also the evidence that Paul allowed women in ministry, defined them in ministerial terms, and, further, required submission to their leadership.

Long ago, Adolph von Harnack presented his theory to explain the changes in social attitudes from Jesus' followers and the earliest expression of the church to Christianity as represented by the Pastoral Epistles (1 and 2 Timothy and Titus). He observed the following progression: (1) the radical perspectives of Jesus, (2) unconventional freedom for women in the earliest congregations, (3) conditional appeals to the cultural norms by use of the household codes, and (4) uncritical acceptance of Graeco-Roman values. He

---

31. Kroeger and Kroeger, *I Suffer Not a Woman,* 14.

called this progression a Hellenization process (that is, a process of being made Greek).[32]

While Harnack's theory is too simplistic, his observation of a gradual Hellenization of the early church has merit. This is best observed when we recall Jewish traditions about slavery. As the people of God, the Jews were commanded never to forget that they were once slaves. In fact, the central story of the Torah (first five books of the Old Testament) is the Exodus, wherein God freed the Hebrew slaves from their Egyptian masters. Therefore, slavery was conditioned by many protections in Israel. Slaves were to be freed in their seventh year of service; moreover, they were to be released with blessings and liberal provisions for livelihood (Ex 21:1–6; Deut 15:12–18). Slavery was not to become a perpetual institution. There was no elitism involved, which reveals quite a different worldview from Aristotle's concept of a natural created hierarchy of superior and inferior.

Careful study of the household codes reveals a very different understanding of their use in the New Testament than is claimed by some popular teachers today. While the appeal to the codes in the New Testament may include "reversion to convention,"[33] the motivation for their use in the New Testament was pragmatic concern, not reinforcement of a concept of natural order in creation. Some popular interpretations of these codes today are more Aristotelian than Christian and ignore the impact of the spiritual qualifications placed on them by the New Testament writers.

Argument from Creation Accounts

The account of Genesis 1:26–31 presents a creation in which male and female are both created in the image of God (cf. 5:1–2). Both are to "have dominion." A second creation account (Gen 2), in which woman is created, includes two references that have been used to promote a hierarchical model of creation. First, in chapter 2, woman is created *after* man and is taken from his rib. Some

---

32. Balch, "Early Christian Criticism."
33. Pagels, "Paul and Women," 546.

believe that priority of appearance indicates superiority. While it might be said that the apostle Paul's words in 1 Corinthians 2 argue an order of priority from this text, the Genesis text does little to support a model of dominance and subordination. The rib symbolizes correspondence between man and woman. The man and the woman belong to each other in a qualitatively different way than they belong to the animals, none of which corresponded to Adam: "There was not found a helper as his partner" (2:20 NRSV). "The unique closeness of her relationship to the man is underlined above all through the fact that she is created, not from the earth but out of the rib from man himself."[34] If anything, the woman is being distinguished not from the man but from the animals, who are not suitable for relationship with the man and are subordinate to him. The woman's superiority for relationship with the man (over the animals), not her inferiority in relationship to the man, is the point of the account.

The second aspect of the text sometimes used to support male dominance is that woman was created to be a "helper" (*ezer*) for man (Gen 2:20). Yet this term, *helper*, is most often used elsewhere in the Old Testament in reference to God. He is the *helper* in his relation to humankind (e.g., Ex 18:4; Isa 30:5; Ps 146:5). If there is any connotation of superiority in this text, the helper, not the one being helped, is superior. There is no connotation of subordination in the term and it should not be used to argue that women should be servile to men.

The concept of subordination first comes up in Genesis 3:16, as a consequence of the fall. Speculation about the weakness, wrongness, or inferiority of women based on this text is a late development in Judaism, occurring first in the second century BC. "The Old Testament [itself] does not emphasize the subordination of wives."[35] The subordination of women is a consequence of the fall. Should God's intention in creation be lifted up as the ideal, or should subordination resulting from the fall? It seems obvious that

---

34. Wolff, *Anthropology of the New Testament*, 94.
35. Balch, "Hellenization / Acculturation in 1 Peter," 97.

subordination is part of the fallen creation, the old order, which according to the apostle Paul is passing away (2 Cor 5:17). Clearly Jewish culture was patriarchal, especially in Jesus' day. Yet women were generally accorded more value in Jewish culture than in the Roman world. Misogynism (extreme devaluation of women) was a late Jewish rabbinical development later adopted by some of the church fathers of the second and third centuries. Such attitudes cannot be based on Scripture's creation accounts.

The Eschatological Age of the Spirit

Another line of investigation in the discussion of women in ministry makes reference to Joel's prophesy quoted by Peter on the day of Pentecost (Acts 2). The implications of this prophesy are developed by the apostle Paul in his teaching of the new creation, the new Adam (Romans 5), and a new Israel—all eschatological (endtimes) categories.

The apostle Paul develops the idea of a new time in which "we are no longer under the law," the time when "faith has come" (Gal 3:25). In his teaching, Paul writes of the inception of that faith and baptism into Christ. In Christ, Paul declares, "There is neither Jew nor Greek, slave nor free, male nor female, for you are all one in Christ Jesus" (here "in Christ" is in the corporate sense of the church, Gal 3:28 NIV1984). The threefold social divisions of this verse correspond to formulas popular in Jewish and Graeco-Roman cultures that maintained such distinctions. The typical morning prayer of the Jewish male in Paul's day included thanksgiving that he was not created a Gentile, a slave, or a woman.[36] Against the Roman household codes and the Jewish man's prayer, the apostle Paul proclaims the dissolution of all such realities. Such an understanding is more than simply a visionary or "spiritual" ideal; it was exactly these distinctions that were addressed in the life and practice of the early church. For example, Peter's vision recorded in Acts 10 was lived out in Caesarea and was the subsequent motivation for inclusion of the Gentiles in the church (Acts 15; cf. Acts 2). The

---

36. Stern, *Daily Prayers.*

unity for which Paul campaigns is to be a practical and practiced reality (Eph 2). Not only does Paul insist that the church live out such a vision, but he also attempts himself to do just that. That is why he confronts Peter (Gal 2:11–14). His practice of recognizing women in ministry, insisting on respect and care for them (Rom 16:1–2), identifying one as his benefactor, one as an elder, another as a teacher, and another as an apostle, are culminating expressions of his conviction that "in Christ, all things are made new" (2 Cor. 5:17). Nevertheless, "whereas Paul's ban on discrimination on racial or social grounds has been widely accepted...there has been a tendency to restrict the degree to which there is no 'male and female.'"[37] While the context of Paul's declaration in Galatians may be limited to a discussion of baptism, which is open to all (as opposed to male circumcision as the sign of the law), these words shaped all early church practices and challenged social division in the church for centuries.

Given the evidence, we must recognize the full implications of "there is neither Jew nor Greek, slave nor free, male nor female, for you are all one in Christ Jesus":

> ...the denial of discrimination which is sacramentally affirmed in baptism holds good for the new existence "in Christ" in its entirety...No more restriction is implied in Paul's equalizing of the status of male and female in Christ than in his equalizing status of Jew and Gentile, of slave and free person. If in ordinary life existence in Christ is manifested openly in church fellowship, if a Gentile may exercise spiritual leadership in church as freely as a Jew, or a slave as freely as a citizen, why not a woman as freely as a man?[38]

Theological Synthesis

The evidence selected and analyzed in this chapter creates a cumulative argument for the inclusion of women, not only actively in the

---

37. Bruce, *Epistle to the Galatians*, 189.
38. Ibid., 190.

life of the church, but also in the function of ministry of the church. The visionary expression of Jesus' life and ministry with women infers it. The practice and expressions of mutuality by the apostle Paul indicate the same. The household codes are best thought of as cultural expressions, appealed to for pragmatic concerns, and in their qualification and amendment by biblical authors indicate an open future. The appeals to creation order are not conclusive as Bill Gothard and others would have us believe and do not support the exclusion of women in ministry. Finally, the idealism of the eschatological age, the age of the Spirit, was certainly understood to have come into being at Pentecost. The implications were gradually recognized and affirmed in the life and practice of the church. The record of the New Testament is the story of that dynamic, and sometimes conflicted, process.

Biblical Precedents for Women in Ministry

Some Christians, in an attempt to allow for women in ministry but also to apply the restrictions of the Pastoral Epistles, offer convoluted attempts to harmonize material in Scripture that appears contradictory. Some argue that women may function in ministry but not with the formal legitimatization of an office, title, or post. A derivation of this idea is that women may be allowed the legitimization of an office, but only where they will not be over men. In such cases, a woman always functions under the authority (and supervision) of a man. Such approaches indicate poor interpretation and synthesis of the biblical texts, and the distinctions drawn between forms of ministry are artificial. Given the varied and comparatively late history of differentiation between clergy and laity, and the late development of offices of ministry, even the Catholic Biblical Association's Committee on the Role of Women in Early Christianity makes the following observation:

> In the primitive Church...ministries were complex and in flux, and the different services later incorporated into the priestly ministry were performed by various members of the

community...Thus, while Paul could speak of charismas as varying in importance...the New Testament evidence does not indicate that one group controlled or exercised all ministries in the earliest Church. Rather the responsibility for ministry, or service, was shared...The Christian priesthood as we know it began to be established no earlier than the end of the first or the beginning of the second century.[39]

The CBA committee recognized that all members of the Body were gifted for up-building ministries (Eph 4:12; cf. vv 11–16; 1 Cor 12:7; 12-31; Rom 12:4–5). Women in the New Testament church did perform ministry and exercise functions that were later defined by offices of ministry. Therefore, the committee concluded *against their own church traditions* (not ordaining women) that "the New Testament evidence, while not decisive by itself, points toward the admission of women to priestly ministry."[40]

Nowhere does the New Testament speak explicitly of women formally in church office. Only three discussions in the New Testament even touch on the participation of women in worship services, and the basic concern of these texts is for proper conduct. First Corinthians 14 cannot mean that women are not to pray and prophesy (preach) in public assembly (cf. 1 Cor 11:3–6). Likewise, what looks like a prohibition of women in congregational leadership in 1 Timothy 2:11–15 runs counter to the evidence of other texts in Scripture.

The household codes cannot govern the general supervision of all women functioning in ministry in the church. In their contexts, they likely apply to husbands and their wives and are concerned with proper interpersonal relations in the family (and perhaps to that particular family in their experience in worship). A further point is that if the apostle Paul were applying the household codes to ministerial function and office in the church, he never would have mentioned Priscilla's name first in his references to her and

---

39. Catholic Biblical Association's Committee on the Role of Women, "Women and Priestly Ministry," 613.

40. Ibid.

her husband. He was already breaking tradition to mention her name at all and to list her as a teacher of Apollos. It makes little sense for Paul to identify women as leaders by the same titles and references that he uses for men and then make absolute statements that disallow women in ministry. Such attempts to reconcile the evidence defy logic and denigrate the texts, which are records of the difficulties encountered when the church lived by a different vision and value system than the surrounding culture. It is far better to understand each text in its literary, social, and historical context.

While the New Testament makes clear the early church's high value of women, we can also see that the general restrictions of the culture were a daily reality, and certain social circumstances led to further restriction. But the same impetus for change regarding the status of women existed in the church as for Gentiles and slaves. The participation of women in services of worship and the inclusion of them in ministry are clear evidence. The prevailing idea that Jesus would return immediately (1 Cor 7) was early motivation to live fearlessly according to the new order, but this was amended in later writings by the desire for tolerance from the dominant cultures. In spite of all the exhortation that the powerless and disadvantaged should accept their plight with grace, the church has never lost the vision of itself as an expression of the kingdom of God, a new reality that recalls Eden and restores shalom. The new creation removes all that divides believers and makes them all—male and female, Jew and Gentile, slave and free—living signs of a new order.

In recognizing women in the function and offices of leadership in the church, the early Church of God (Anderson, Indiana) understood itself as living according to the new realities called into being in Christ. The best understanding of Scripture calls for us to be so visionary today.

About the Author
Sharon Clark Pearson is an ordained minister in the Church of God, Anderson, Indiana. Sharon has served as a minister in

congregational, district, and national settings. She earned her PhD from Fuller Theological Seminary in New Testament studies. Her writings have been published in Church of God literature and other journals, magazines, and books. Dr. Pearson has served as an associate professor of New Testament at Azusa Pacific University and at Anderson University School of Theology. She has also taught undergraduates at Anderson University and graduate students at Southern Wesleyan University.

CHAPTER 4

Women Evangelists in the Church of God at the Beginning of the Twentieth Century

BY SUSIE C. STANLEY

From its inception, the Church of God has affirmed women's call to ministry. It is crucial to be aware of our foremothers. We are blessed with so many of them! They form a cloud of witnesses who can inspire us as we "run with perseverance in the race that is set before us" (Heb 12:1 NRSV).

Women in the Church of God today follow in the footsteps of pioneering women preachers who blazed a trail that has now become overgrown with weeds. Some people have forgotten there ever was a trail. A diminishing number of runners have been able to keep the way barely visible. The path needs to be worn down by women today who answer the call to ordained ministry and follow the path created by our foremothers.

A sample reading of early issues of the *Gospel Trumpet* magazine reveals the significant involvement of Church of God women in evangelistic outreach. For instance, the News from the Field column in the *Gospel Trumpet* recorded information for eighty-eight women active in ministry during the years 1891 and 1892. This chapter briefly documents the early acceptance of women preachers in the Wesleyan-Holiness Movement. Then it will highlight four women evangelists in the Church of God: Mother Sarah Sauer Smith, Mary Cole, Nora Siens Hunter, and Lena Shoffner Matthesen. They were chosen primarily because of their prominence in the Church of God and the availability of resources recounting their ministries.

Wesleyan-Holiness Affirmation of Women in Ministry

The Church of God endorsed and encouraged women to preach during the late nineteenth century at a time when very few denominations ordained women. Why was the Church of God so supportive of women preachers during its early years? The answer lies in its roots within the Wesleyan-Holiness Movement. Sociologist Bryan Wilson notes the positive correlation between Wesleyan-Holiness doctrine and women's public involvement in religious activities:

> The Holiness Movement in its varied forms brought women to the fore, perhaps more than any previous development in Christianity. This was not through the leadership of any one woman, but was a widely diffused tendency...It was the first development in Christianity which admitted them to positions of influence on any wide scale, both because external influences sanctioned and, because the freedom emphasized in the new movement ignored traditional Christian precepts on the subjects.[1]

The Church of God emerged out of the broader Wesleyan-Holiness Movement late in the nineteenth century. This movement, drawing on the theology of John Wesley, promoted the doctrine of

---

1. Wilson, *Religious Sects*, 59-60; Hardesty, *Women Called to Witness*; Hardesty, Dayton, and Dayton, "Women in the Holiness Movement."

holiness, or sanctification, which is understood as a second distinct work of grace following the experience of salvation, the first work of grace. At conversion, a person's sins are forgiven, while sanctification results in purity of heart. Churches that resulted from the Wesleyan-Holiness Movement include the Salvation Army, the Wesleyan Church, the Free Methodist Church, and the Church of the Nazarene.

Phoebe Palmer, a Methodist laywoman, popularized Wesleyan-Holiness doctrine in the United States.[2] Her preaching and writing ministry extended from the late 1830s until her death in 1874. She based her doctrine of holiness on John Wesley's writings, which gave the movement its name. Palmer insisted that a sanctified person must testify publicly to the experience of holiness or it could be lost. As a result of this requirement, many women spoke in public for the first time. Since the distance from testifying to preaching is a short one, many women in the Wesleyan-Holiness Movement became evangelists.

The understanding of the source of ministerial authority in the Wesleyan-Holiness Movement also contributed to the acceptance of women as preachers. The Wesleyan-Holiness Movement affirmed women in leadership positions because of its emphasis on the Holy Spirit. It ascribed authority to the Holy Spirit rather than to the priestly office, where authority is transmitted by ecclesiastical leadership. Women generally hold prominent positions in groups which derive authority from the Holy Spirit. The Spirit is no respecter of persons but dispenses gifts of ministry to both men and women. F. G. Smith, an early leader in the Church of God, articulated this prophetic view of authority in a letter to a "sister in Christ":

Again, I call your attention to the organization of the church by the Holy Spirit. A man is an evangelist because he has the gift of evangelizing. It is not because he is a man, but because he has that particular gift. The gift itself is the proof of his calling.

2. Charles White, *Beauty of Holiness*; Raser, *Phoebe Palmer*.

If a woman has divine gifts fitting her for a particular work in the church, that is the proof, and the only proof needed, that that is her place. Any other basis of qualification than divine gifts is superficial and arbitrary and ignores the divine plan of organization and government in the church.[3]

Other Church of God authors also emphasized that the Holy Spirit dispenses gifts equally among women and men.[4]

Wesleyan-Holiness believers patterned themselves after the early church, sometimes referred to as the primitive church, which also endorsed the work of the Holy Spirit. Wesleyan-Holiness adherents documented the role of women in the Bible and sought to restore to women the place they had initially held in the church. Luther Lee, a founder of the Wesleyan Church, argued: "All antiquity agrees that there were female officers and teachers in the Primitive Church."[5]

Grounded firmly in the Wesleyan-Holiness tradition, the Church of God affirmed women in ministry because it stressed the authority of the Holy Spirit, who gifts both men and women to serve in all capacities of religious work. By so doing, leaders believed they were modeling themselves after the early church.

Empowerment Equips Women for Ministry

Empowerment accompanies the experience of sanctification. Wesleyan-Holiness leaders such as Phoebe Palmer traced the doctrine to the day of Pentecost, when the first Christians received God's power. Jesus had instructed his followers to stay in Jerusalem "until you have been clothed with power from on high" (Luke 24:49 NRSV). Palmer proclaimed, "Holiness is power."[6] Wesleyan-Holiness women attributed the power which accompanied sanctification to the Holy Spirit. It was this power which enabled women to overcome any hesitation about preaching and which sustained them

3. F. G. S. [Smith], "Editorial," *Gospel Trumpet*, October 14, 1920, 2.

4. For instance, Bishop, "Should Women Preach?"; Cole, "Labor of Women in the Gospel."

5. Lee, "Woman's Right to Preach," 88–91.

6. Palmer, *Promise of the Father*, 206.

when anyone questioned their right to preach. Equipped with the empowerment of the Holy Spirit, women challenged the popular misconception that said it was unwomanly to speak in public.

Empowerment by the Holy Spirit often resulted in a dramatic personality change. Women lost their timidity when they were sanctified.[7] Holy Spirit power transformed timidity into "holy boldness." Phoebe Palmer and others used this phrase to describe their newfound courage resulting from sanctification.[8]

Empowerment also enabled women to overcome the "man-fearing spirit" that initially may have caused them to restrict their religious activities. Women sometimes reported that prior to sanctification they had allowed fear of opposition to stifle them. Mother Sarah Smith described her experience of sanctification: "I was filled with the power and the Holy Ghost and such boldness. All that man-fearing spirit was taken away, and my heart was overflowing with perfect love that was so unspeakable and full of glory."[9] The power that accompanied the experience of sanctification enabled women to crush the paralyzing "man-fearing spirit" and begin to preach.

The Biblical Basis for Women in Ministry

The interpretation of the Bible by early Wesleyan-Holiness leaders endorsed women's right to preach. Advocates in other denominations such as Phoebe Palmer and B. T. Roberts, a founder of the Free Methodist Church, wrote books providing biblical support for women clergy. Alma White, founder of the Pillar of Fire denomination, and William Godbey, a prominent evangelist, are among those who authored pamphlets on the topic.[10] Church of God

---

7. Phoebe Palmer, Alma White, and Sarah Smith are three examples. (Loveland, "Domesticity and Religion," 259, 261; Stanley, *Feminist Pillar of Fire*, 24; Sarah Smith, "Autobiography," 305.)

8. Palmer, *Way of Holiness*, 85, 33. See also Stanley, *Holy Boldness*, 94–95, 99; this book analyzes thirty-four American Wesleyan-Holiness women, including Church of God women Mary Cole and Sarah Sauer Smith.

9. Sarah Smith, *Life Sketches of Mother Sarah Smith*, 16.

10. Palmer, *Promise of the Father*; Roberts, *Ordaining Women*; Alma White, *Woman's Ministry*.

interpretations of scriptures relating to women in ministry paralleled these Wesleyan-Holiness defenses.[11]

Grounded in the experience of Pentecost, the Wesleyan-Holiness hermeneutic supporting women clergy also focused on Galatians 3:28 and Psalm 68:11, and incorporated the accounts of prominent women in the Bible who provided models for women preachers.

At Pentecost, the divine commission was addressed to both sexes. This event documented women's ministry. Pentecost served as the precedent for women's leadership in the church. Mary Cole, who incorporated a brief defense of women preachers in her autobiography, pointed out that Acts 1:14 documents the presence of women, including Jesus' mother, at Pentecost. Acts 2:4 records that they all spoke as the Spirit gave them utterance. Cole asked, "Does not the 'all' include the women present? Was not their speaking as the Spirit gave utterance the act of a minister in preaching?"[12] To Cole, the answer to both questions was an unqualified yes.

B. T. Roberts urged that Scripture used to oppose women preachers should be measured against the standard of Galatians 3:28: "Make this the KEY TEXT upon this subject, and give to other passages such a construction as will make them agree with it, and all is harmony."[13] F. G. Smith's view corresponded with Roberts's sentiment. He referred to Galatians 3:28 as an "expression of basic principles" which "boldly declared a different standard for the kingdom of God."[14] Other Church of God authors also employed Galatians 3:28 in their defenses of women's ministry.[15] Many Wesleyan-Holiness leaders quoted with favor Adam Clarke's translation of Psalm 68:11, "of the female preachers there was a great host."[16]

---

11. For several examples, see Bishop, "Should Women Preach?" *Gospel Trumpet*, June 17, 1920, 8–9; C. E. Brown, "Women Preachers," *Gospel Trumpet*, 5, 13; Cole, "Labor of Women in the Gospel," 1.

12. Mary Cole, *Trials and Triumphs of Faith*, 87.

13. Roberts, *Ordaining Women*, 55. See Stanley "Galatians 3:28," 179–86, for further information on the use of Galatians 3:28 to support women preachers.

14. F. G. S. [Smith], Editorial, 1.

15. For example, see Bishop, "Should Women Preach?," 9; Brown, "Women Preachers," 5.

16. Clarke, *Holy Bible*, 3:342.

Wesleyan-Holiness writers claimed that the prophecy declared by this verse was being fulfilled by women in the Wesleyan-Holiness Movement. Nora Hunter, whose life and ministry is profiled in this chapter, frequently quoted Psalm 68:11.

Supporters of women clergy in the Wesleyan-Holiness Movement noticed that the ministry of Jesus also corroborated women's public ministries. Alma White often mentioned the woman of Samaria in her sermons because she illustrates Jesus' approval of women's ministry.[17] The events surrounding Jesus' death and resurrection also provided evidence for Wesleyan-Holiness arguments favoring women in ministry. The popular refrain that women were "last at the cross, and earliest at the grave" was often invoked.

Wesleyan-Holiness interpreters pointed out the ministry of women in the book of Acts and women who were co-workers with Paul. Mary Cole drew attention to Phoebe, whom Paul commends in Romans 16:1. Rather than challenging the mistranslation of *diakonos* as "servant," Cole took another tack. In response to those who argued that this verse restricts women's role in the church to domestic work, Cole argued:

> If the inference of this scripture is that a woman can serve the church by doing temporal [secular] work only, the preachers are not doing their duty, because in the second verse the Lord commanded the other ministers to assist Phoebe. If then the women's only service be to cook for the ministers, the ministers, if they would obey this scripture, should certainly help the women cook.[18]

In summary, several factors contributed to the acceptance of women in ministry in the Wesleyan-Holiness Movement: the requirement that all persons publicly testify regarding their experience of sanctification, the emphasis on the Holy Spirit, and the Wesleyan-Holiness interpretation of Scripture. Like other

---

17. For example, Alma White, *Story of My Life*, 3:360.
18. Mary Cole, *Trials and Triumphs of Faith*, 87.

prophetic religious groups, the Wesleyan-Holiness Movement encouraged women to defy the traditional stereotype that a woman's place is in the home and that precluded women's leadership in religious activities.

Biographies of Women Evangelists

Mother Sarah Sauer Smith

Mother Sarah Sauer Smith wrote a brief autobiography, *Life Sketches,* in 1901. Born on September 20, 1822, in Summit County, Ohio, Sarah Sauer received only three months of formal education, first at a German school when she was twelve and later at an English school. She described her childhood briefly: "I was raised strictly moral."[19]

Smith recounted her conversion experience in 1842: "While the clock was striking nine, I sprang to my feet a new woman. Oh, how God did fill my soul with joy and glory and such sweet peace that I walked the floor praising God!"[20] Neither her parents nor her church shared Sarah's newfound joy. Her parents forbade her to go to prayer meetings or to pray in secret. Sarah was further dismayed that the Lutheran church of her birth refused to let her pray in the church service. She was eventually cast out of the Lutheran church.

Smith experienced sanctification in 1859, though it wasn't until four years later that she first heard that term used to describe it. Smith related the struggle that ensued as she sought sanctification. "I could say yes to everything until God said, 'Are you willing to work for me?' Then the devil saw his last chance and said, 'If you promise to work for God you will have to leave home, and your husband will not let you go.'"[21] Mother Smith recalled that "the death struggle commenced." The victory was hers. Smith reported that friends were astonished at the change in her personality as a result of sanctification, which transformed her fear into boldness.

---

19. Sarah Smith, *Life Sketches of Mother Sarah Smith*, 3.
20. Ibid., 6.
21. Ibid., 16.

In Jerry City, Ohio, Sarah Smith led a group of thirty-five people who met four times a week in a holiness association. Smith first learned of D. S. (Daniel Sydney) Warner, a prominent leader during the early years of the Church of God, through his writings. Someone sent her one of his first papers, including an article on "The One Church." Smith agreed with Warner's position: "I would not dare to say a word against it, for that was just what I was looking for."[22] Warner and those who joined him rejected denominations, separating themselves from their former affiliations. The goal was that all Christians would follow this example, forming the one true church. Warner and a colleague, Alexander J. Kilpatrick, visited Smith's group in 1882. As a result, twenty people stood to declare their freedom from sectarianism, including Sarah Smith, who asked that her name be removed from both the class book of the Methodist Episcopal Church, which she had joined, and from a United Brethren holiness band book.[23] After that, Smith frequently wrote for the *Gospel Trumpet,* detailing her evangelistic work in Ohio.[24]

Once she had declared her freedom from all denominational affiliations, Smith wrestled with another decision:

> The Lord began to show me that I must break up housekeeping and go into the gospel work...I said I was too old, as my age was 61, and I have no education but the Lord told me what to do. I said who will take care of my husband? He said the children and He would care for him...That evening I went home and told my folks what I would do, and in ten days I was on my way, cut loose from house and home, not knowing whether I would even see my home again.[25]

Smith shared her decision with her husband at the breakfast table. He finished eating his breakfast, walked out and then returned,

---

22. Ibid., 23.
23. Sarah Smith, "Fifty Years in the Kingdom of Heaven."
24. Allison, "Life of D. S. Warner," 13.
25. Sarah Smith, *Life Sketches of Mother Sarah Smith,* 26, 28, 30.

asking how soon she would have to leave. When his wife replied she would leave in ten days or two weeks, he responded, "I will get you some money." He obtained the money by selling a cow.[26] One wonders what else transpired between the two; just one brief paragraph in her account covers the conversation.

Mother Smith headed for Beaver Dam, Indiana, where she met D. S. Warner, Barney Warren, Frances (Frankie) Miller, and Nannie Kigar. The five of them composed the first evangelistic company of the Church of God. Smith sang high tenor in the quartet. Her responsibilities also included testifying, praying, and occasional preaching. She was known for her glowing testimonies, during which she sometimes shouted, clapped, and even jumped.[27] The company formed in 1885 and worked together for more than four years, holding meetings in ten states and Canada. In each location, whether a church or a brush arbor outside, they "preached the whole truth—justification, sanctification, one church, and divine healing."[28]

Looking back, Mother Smith recalled that God protected the company from mobs in several cities. At Grover, Indiana, opponents showered them with eggs, but no one was hit. The company never took up a collection during their travels, but relied on God to supply their needs. Mother Smith reported that the members of the company worked well together: "We were all of one heart and one mind and saw eye to eye."[29] Warner's company provided a model for "flying ministries," which offered the opportunity for many women to serve as evangelists.[30] How did a woman of Smith's age endure traveling by lumber wagon and other conveyances of the late 1800s? No complaints appear in her sketches. Mother Smith's strength, both physical and spiritual, must have been phenomenal.

Mother Smith's spirit and enthusiasm inspired others. Mary Cole recalled, "Mother Sarah Smith, who sat right in front of the

26. Ibid., 31; Byers, "Pioneers of the Present Reformation: Sketch No. 4," 5.

27. John W. V. Smith, *Quest for Holiness and Unity*, 72.

28. Sarah Smith, "Autobiography," 312.

29. Sarah Smith, *Life Sketches of Mother Sarah Smith*, 34.

30. John W. V. Smith, *Quest for Holiness and Unity*, 73.

pulpit and who always encouraged the ministers and held up their hands with her 'Amen! Praise the Lord.'"[31] Mother Smith's obituary in the *Gospel Trumpet* summarized her ministry:

> She has for many years been a faithful mother in Israel. Wherever she was known, she was known as "Mother Smith." She was known not only by that name, but she was known to be a firebrand for God and a terror to Satan. For more than 20 years she has attended various camp-meetings of the saints, and during this time she was widely known…Her testimonies were generally so inspiring as to set the camp-meeting blazing as it were, with the praises and manifestations of the glory of God… While she has gone to her reward above, the church on earth has lost a staunch advocate of the full gospel in this evening of time.[32]

Just as Deborah arose as a mother in Israel (see Judg 5:7), Sarah Smith arose in the early days of the Church of God to inspire and encourage others to participate in the work of the Lord.

Mary Cole

Mary Cole was born on a farm outside Decatur, Iowa, on August 23, 1853. She was the seventh of twelve children, eight boys and four girls. When she was one, her family moved to Illinois. Two years later, they moved to Missouri, where Mary spent the rest of her childhood and young adulthood. Health problems plagued her from the age of two when she began having spasms. By the age of fifteen, she was an invalid, spending five months at a time in bed.

At the age of seventeen, Mary joined the Methodist Episcopal Church, South, on probation, but her conversion didn't occur until the next year on May 3, 1871. She first heard about the doctrine of sanctification four weeks after her conversion from her oldest brother, Jeremiah, who was a minister. She sought and attained the

---

31. Mary Cole, *Trials and Triumphs of Faith*, 52–53.
32. "Mother Smith Goes to Rest," *Gospel Trumpet*, March 12, 1903, 8.

experience the same day Jeremiah talked to her: "When I received the sanctifying grace, I did not think of demonstration, or of great feeling, or of anything of that kind: I simply consecrated all a living sacrifice, and reckoned myself dead indeed unto sin and alive unto God through our Lord Jesus Christ. I met the conditions and believed that the word was done."[33]

At the age of twenty-two, Mary attended a camp meeting sponsored by several denominations. It was there God said to her, "Go preach My gospel." Mary responded by making excuses: "Lord, I am not talented; my education is so meager [sic]; there is no one to go with me; and besides, I have a stammering tongue."[34] Mary returned home and reported God's will for her future to her Methodist Episcopal class leader. He responded by saying, "You are a pretty looking thing to be called to preach." Mary recorded that she agreed with his assessment, but she didn't know what to say, so she replied, "I do not believe that every one called to preach will have to stand in the pulpit; a person may preach by his life and conduct."[35] At this point, it appears she was unwilling to defend her calling.

Mary was engaged to be married at age twenty-six, but she broke off the engagement when God made it clear to her that she should not marry. In her memoirs, she does not mention the young man's name. Again, we can only wonder about the unspoken. What agony did it cause Mary to break the engagement? Did she ever regret the decision? How did her fiancé take the news? She remained single the rest of her life.

Nearly seven years elapsed before Mary acted on her calling. In the interim, she was miraculously healed in the fall of 1880. God also cured her stammering to the extent that it did not interfere when she preached. Mary received the gift of exhortation accompanied by the Spirit's power when she was healed. The first meeting she mentions was in Wymore, Nebraska, with her brother George and Sister Lodema Kaser. She preached her first sermon at a Holiness convention held in Salisbury, Missouri. The minister in charge

---

33. Mary Cole, *Trials and Triumphs of Faith*, 14.

34. Ibid., 51.

35. Ibid., 52–53.

of the service got up and announced that God had not given him a message. He further admonished that if the person who had the message did not deliver it, that person would be responsible to God. Although ministers and workers were sitting all around her, Mary jumped to her feet immediately: "I had a message from heaven—burning words that went right into the hearts of the people. God made my tongue as the pen of a ready writer. The power of God was on me in such measure that I could hardly tell whether I was in heaven or on earth."[36] Mary often spoke of the divine power which made her preaching possible.

Mary reported that in her early evangelistic work, there was considerable opposition to her preaching. At nearly every meeting, she had to explain the scriptural view on the matter of women preachers, responding to 1 Corinthians 14:35 and 1 Timothy 2:12, two texts which opponents claimed as proof that women should not preach. Mary would point out that they were misusing Scripture to support their false position.

For three years, Mary and her brother Jeremiah worked in Missouri, preaching in school houses for two to four weeks' duration. Sometimes, they would separate and hold two meetings simultaneously in different locations. In these revivals, she preached twice a day and three times on Sunday.

During her early ministry, Mary remained in the Methodist Episcopal Church, which did not license women at that time. On first receiving the *Gospel Trumpet*, she burned it and wrote to Warner advising him she didn't wish to receive any more copies. She was offended by the group's opposition to the licensing of preachers. Even though her own denomination refused to license her, Mary approved of ministerial licensing. Initially, she also opposed the rejection of denominationalism. She believed that individuals who had experienced holiness and remained in their denominations would make their churches better. This was the position of many Methodists. D. S. Warner obviously forgave Mary for her early aversion to the movement since he wrote favorably of her in

---

36. Ibid., 84.

his diary, calling her "a chosen and anointed instrument of God to preach and testify the Gospel of the grace of God."[37]

Mary eventually left the Methodist Episcopal Church by sending for her membership letter and then tearing it up. She does not share what made her change her mind, though she does tell about an experience that occurred the previous summer at the quarterly conference of the denomination. She had been asked to conduct meetings in conjunction with the conference. During one of the services, the ministers met secretly and decided to stop her meetings. Mary was heartbroken: "I could not keep from crying. I had called the Methodist Church my mother; and now to think that my mother was treating me in this way, made me feel very bad."[38]

Mary Cole also faced rumors intended to hinder her ministry. One rumor claimed she was one of the James Boys, the notorious outlaws, disguised as a woman. One wonders what the other rumors were!

Mary spoke of the helpfulness and encouragement women evangelists offered each other. She wrote of Mother Smith's personal support, "Mother Smith was quite helpful, as the enemy tried to depress and crush."[39] Sister Bolds also was a great encouragement to Mary. Mary had an opportunity to assist other women as well. Once, she felt led to visit a woman in Iowa who was "going through some deep trials." She describes the problem this colleague was having:

> Her difficulty seemed to be mainly self-accusation. In other words, she had set her spiritual standard so high that she could not live up to her own ideal...Some of God's dear little ones who are very conscientious, sometimes look upon the Lord as a severe father. It seems to them that he, like Pharaoh, wants them to make brick without straw, to gather stubble. With this idea of God in mind, they have a hard time and fail to see him

---

37. As quoted in Byers, *Birth of a Reformation*. Anderson, IN: Gospel Trumpet, 1921, 354.
38. Mary Cole, *Trials and Triumphs of Faith*, 124–25.
39. Ibid., 189, 147.

as a good, kind, loving heavenly Father, one whose heart is overflowing with mercy and compassion for his dear tired children, ready to make a way for their escape.[40]

On another occasion, Mary visited Sioux Falls, South Dakota, to spend time with a colleague "who was needing some special encouragement."[41]

Mary writes of troubles during her services. Once, someone put red pepper on the stove located in the center of the room; the fumes from it nearly stifled the congregation. Twice during the same series of meetings, eggs were thrown at the workers, but none hit them. At a camp meeting in Mole Hill, West Virginia, a mob appeared, threatening to tear the tent down. Shots were exchanged between the mob and those who were defending the worshipers. Mary admitted later, that as bullets whizzed near her, she ducked behind the canvas for protection. Afterward, she laughed at herself for seeking such a flimsy refuge.

Preachers at some camp meetings at that time had an unusual method of determining who would bring the message. The first person to reach the pulpit at the appointed time was the one who preached. During the service at a camp meeting in Michigan, God made it clear to Mary that she should deliver the evening message:

> I submitted the matter to the Lord, telling him that if he still wanted me to deliver the message, to hold the brother back until it would not appear that I was trying to get ahead of him. God wonderfully owned and blessed his Word, and a number of backsliders were reclaimed. After the service, the brother who had thought he had the message came to me and said, "Sister Cole, I did think I had the message, but the Lord blessed you." "Yes," I said, "The Lord blessed me in obeying but it took more grace than usual."[42]

---

40. Ibid., 270.
41. Ibid., 272.
42. Ibid., 190.

It took not only an extra measure of grace but the speed of an Olympic sprinter! She had traveled far from her timid response to the leader who tried to discourage her when she was first called to preach.

Mary conducted services in Missouri and Kansas. She also mentions holding camp meetings in Nebraska, Oklahoma, Indiana, Illinois, West Virginia, and Michigan. The greater part of her work in later years was with her younger brother, George, who first joined her in 1890. They conducted services in twelve states.[43] Lodema Kaser also accompanied Mary over a period of seven years.[44]

Mary and a company of six others traveled to California in 1894, holding services in Los Angeles, San Francisco, and Fresno. In Los Angeles, most of the company was under arrest for about three hours for preaching on the street. Mary does not mention if she was one of those arrested. After working in California for sixteen months, the company headed back East, stopping in Arizona for meetings in Phoenix.

Mary and her brother George settled in Chicago in 1898. They assisted there for one year before assuming responsibility for the rescue mission. The mission offered overnight lodging for five cents, which included a free breakfast.[45] During her first winter in Chicago, Mary helped with meetings for homeless men in the slum district and conducted cottage meetings in private homes. In March 1903, workers began building a home and chapel, which was finished by Christmas. This facility became the model for other missionary homes.[46] Mary spent ten years in Chicago before moving to Anderson to care for her mother in the old folks' home there. Mary died in the Anderson Old People's Home on August 27, 1940.

---

43. George L. Cole, Autobiography, 349.

44. Byers, "Pioneers of the Present Reformation: Sketch No. 3," 23. Kaser joined Mary and George later in Chicago and assisted in the mission work there for four years (Byers, "Pioneers of the Present Reformation: Sketch No. 12," 5–6).

45. George L. Cole, Autobiography, 351.

46. John W. V. Smith, Quest for Holiness and Unity, 232.

Nora Siens Hunter

While the name of Nora Siens Hunter now is associated with the origin and early years of the missionary work of the women of the Church of God, she began her ministry as an evangelist.[47]

Nora Siens was born on August 15, 1873, in Kansas. When her mother died nine years later, her father placed Nora and her brother in a Soldier's Orphanage, where Nora remained for five years. She then lived near Galesburg, Kansas, with relatives for two years. It was at the Meeker school house in Galesburg under the preaching of Dr. S. G. Bryant that Nora experienced conversion in 1892. Bryant himself had been converted under the ministry of the company which included Mary Cole and Lodema Kaser.[48] Nora joined the Bryants, traveling with them for one year in evangelistic work, primarily assisting in the area of music and personal work. Then she worked with William Smith and his wife, S. J. Smith, for several months. During the summer of 1893, she and another woman gave oversight to the Children's Home adjacent to the Gospel Trumpet Company publishing plant, then located in Grand Junction, Michigan.

Nora probably preached her first sermon that summer in Grand Junction. It was after D. S. Warner's encouragement that Nora began preaching at the age of nineteen. Warner, who was in the audience at Grand Junction, asked Nora to join his company, which at the time consisted of himself, his new wife (the former Frankie Miller), and F. G. and Birdie Smith. Nora traveled with them for about a year.

Nora was involved in the innovative ministry which incorporated the "Floating Bethel," a gospel houseboat built on a flatboat by G. T. Clayton. Workers advertised meetings by putting notices in bottles and throwing them overboard. The intention was to notify towns downstream of their impending arrival.[49] Gospel workers

---

47. Most of the information on Nora Hunter's life is derived from Neal and Bolitho, *Madam President*.

48. John W. V. Smith, *Heralds of a Brighter Day*, 129.

49. Byers, "Pioneers of the Present Reformation: Sketch No. 5," 9.

visited towns located along the Ohio River, distributing literature, holding tent meetings, and visiting the sick.

In the fall of 1894, Nora worked with W. J. and L. E. Henry, conducting services in Indiana and Ohio for two years.[50] After this period of ministry, she met Lena Shoffner and they decided to form a team of two. Nora conducted a meeting with Lena in Federalsburg, Maryland, in the fall of 1895. This meeting was beset by troubles. First, the tent blew down. The two then rented a Quaker church five miles away, which turned out to be infested by hornets that stung the congregation. In spite of all the difficulties, a thriving congregation resulted from Nora and Lena's efforts.

Nora met Clarence Edgar Hunter at the Grand Junction camp meeting. After their marriage on November 3, 1896, the couple traveled together, holding services in various locations. They held several pastorates in Kansas, Indiana, and Pennsylvania before moving to Los Angeles. About 1923, Nora and her husband began prayer meetings and Sunday schools in private homes. A year and a half later, when the group formed a congregation, Nora became the pastor. She cooperated with the East Los Angeles Health Center by assisting the homeless in locating housing and helping newcomers find jobs and food. During this time, she served on a government censoring board which was responsible for assessing moving, was a member of the California Conference on Child Health and Protection, and chaired the State Committee on Character Education.[51]

A five-month trip to Europe and the Middle East in 1929 led Nora to organize the Woman's Home and Foreign Missionary Society. Founded in 1932, the name of the group is now Christian Women Connection. Nora served as president from 1932 to 1948, maintaining a busy schedule. One summer she attended nineteen camp meetings. She retired from active involvement in 1948 and died on January 27, 1951. Known as "the church's sweetheart," Nora Hunter left a legacy which continues to be an avenue through

---

50. "New from the Field," *Gospel Trumpet*, December 27, 1894, 3.
51. John W. V. Smith, *Heralds of a Brighter Day*, 143.

which women reach out to the people for whom Hunter carried so great a burden.

Lena Schoffner Matthesen

Lena Shoffner was born on February 26, 1868, near Nishnabotna, Atchinson County, Missouri. She describes her upbringing briefly in a short account of her life: "I had a very pious training from my parents. They forbade my going to worldly amusements, such as theaters, balls, and card and wine parties. Neither would they allow me to read novels or continued stories of any kind."[52] As a young working woman, she succumbed to the influence of those around her and abandoned her parents' strict standards. She came under conviction, which resulted in conversion in February 1886. It was not until four years later when she attended a meeting held by D. S. Warner and company that she experienced sanctification.

Before that time, Lena felt that God wanted her to preach, but she did not understand what her specific role should be. Insight came in 1892: God wanted her to become an evangelist. She left her family in January, expecting to be gone ten days—but two years passed before she saw them again. Her schedule of meetings took her from Arkansas City, Kansas, to Grand Junction, Michigan, and east through Pennsylvania. On November 4, 1893, she embarked for England. She conducted services in Liverpool, London, and Birkenhead before returning to the States on August 31, 1895.

After attending a camp meeting in Pennsylvania, Lena joined Nora Hunter for an evangelistic tour of Maryland during the fall of 1895. (One meeting on that tour was discussed in the section on Nora Hunter.)

Lena is best known for the sermon she preached to an integrated congregation at the 1897 state camp meeting held near Hartselle, Alabama. The group met the legal requirement for segregation of blacks and whites by placing a rope down the middle of the tent, with blacks sitting on one side and whites on the other. Taking as her text Ephesians 2:14 ("For he is our peace, who hath made both

---

52. Shoffner, Autobiography, 336.

one, and hath broken down the middle wall of partition between us," KJV), Lena preached for one and a half hours, a typical length at that time, on the evils of racial prejudice. Her sermon found its mark: someone took down the rope and both races prayed together at the altar.[53]

Lena traveled to Oklahoma with co-worker Mabel Ashenfelter in the spring of 1904 to conduct meetings in Oklahoma City. While preaching one evening, a member of Firebrand, a rival Holiness group, came to the platform and proclaimed: "I rebuke thee in the name of the Lord." The individual claimed Lena was preaching incorrect doctrine and insisted she leave the pulpit. John W. V. Smith recounts what happened next: "She stopped her sermon long enough to place her hand on her hip, look the opposer in the eye and tell him that they had paid rent for the hall and furnished it and if he did not like what he was hearing he could rent a place and preach as he wished."[54] Obviously, the challenger had met his match!

A new congregation resulted from this series of meetings in Oklahoma City. Lena's ministry took on a new dimension when she agreed to conclude her evangelistic work and serve as the first pastor of the congregation with Mable Ashenfelter as her associate. Lena held this position for eight years.[55]

Lena met Ed Matthesen during the revival at Oklahoma City in 1904. They were married later that year. They worked together throughout Oklahoma until her death on October 10, 1936.

Conclusion

The affirmation of women clergy is a distinguishing characteristic of the Wesleyan-Holiness Movement. Wesleyan-Holiness leaders quoted Scripture passages to endorse women's expanded role in the Church and criticized interpretations of verses which purportedly prohibited women's involvement in preaching and other leadership

---

53. John W. E. Smith, *Quest for Holiness and Unity*, 165. This incident is also referenced in Allison, "Heroines of the Faith," 12.

54. Ibid., 129.

55. Hale, "History of the Beginning and Early Years," 45.

activities. The Wesleyan-Holiness Movement encouraged women to preach by claiming it was their Christian duty. Moving beyond rhetoric, Wesleyan-Holiness churches ordained women in unprecedented numbers, facilitating and, at the same time, legitimizing women's fulfillment of their duty to God.

The four women discussed here are representative of hundreds of women in the Church of God who devoted their lives to Christian ministry as evangelists and pastors. These women form a "great cloud of witnesses" who provide inspiration as we "run with perseverance the race that is set before us" (Heb 12:1 NRSV).

About the Author

Susie Stanley has specialized in the history and theology of the Wesleyan-Holiness movement. Over the past thirty-five years, she has lectured and written extensively about the movement, considering topics such as social holiness, sanctified feminism, camp meetings, and the relevance of holiness today. Among her publications are *Feminist Pillar of Fire: The Life of Alma White* and *Holy Boldness*, which incorporates the ministries of thirty-four Wesleyan-Holiness women preachers. Her academic interest in women in ministry is paralleled by her activism, which includes founding and leading Wesleyan/Holiness Women Clergy, International, from 1992 to 2006. Under her leadership, the group promoted and encouraged women clergy by publishing booklets, establishing a mentoring program, and sponsoring conferences. Susie is an ordained minister in the Church of God. She taught twelve years at Western Evangelical Seminary and sixteen years at Messiah College before retiring in 2011. Susie received the Lifetime Achievement Award from the Wesleyan Theological Society in 2012. Susie is married to John. They have two children and three grandchildren.

CHAPTER 5

African American Women in Ministry

BY ARNETTA MCNEESE BAILEY

The roles of African American women in ministry in the Church of God are as diverse as the calling itself. "It was he who gave some to be apostles, some to be prophets, some to be evangelists, and some to be pastors and teachers" (Eph 4:11 NIV1984). James Earl Massey says, "The very mention of African Americans does more than identify a people, their ethnic background and present setting. It is also an index to American history and to the history of the Christian religion in America."[1] African American women have been present in the life of the Church of God from its early beginnings and continue to serve with distinction in every arena of the church. They have taken the baton passed to them by Jane Williams, church planter; Ozzie Wattleton, evangelist; Pansy Brown, educator; Joe Mae Whitehead, business woman; and Addie Wyatt, change agent within the church and beyond.

It is impossible to include in this chapter a comprehensive list of the African American women in ministry and their contributions

---

1. Massey, *African Americans and the Church of God*, 9.

to the church. Their creativity and commitment to the call on their lives has allowed these women to walk with clear purpose and forge new territories of service. The African American women who have dared to answer the call to ministry have become innovators, planters, torch bearers, and grassroots laborers, and have used technology to add a fresh look to the twenty-first century.

This chapter is a celebration of and a tribute to only a fraction of the individuals who have sacrificed and labored in the vineyard. There are 291 ordained and registered African American women listed in the Church of God Yearbook. This number represents, but is not limited to, 69 senior pastors, 123 associate pastors, 19 co-pastors, 9 serving in higher education, 8 ministers of music, 4 who serve as children's pastors, 4 evangelists, and 2 women serving in the ministry of pastoral care.

One such woman, Alice Dise, authored the chapter in the first edition of this book which chronicles African American women ministers in the Church of God. She has continued to provide mentoring and valuable resources for clergywomen in the church. Rev. Dise is an ordained minister of the Church of God and has served the movement as a preacher while also holding local, state, and national offices. She is in demand across denominational lines as a teacher, preacher, and workshop leader, especially in areas of Christian education and women in ministry. She is the author of the student workbook and leader's guide for Dr. Vashti M. McKenzie's book *Journey to the Well* and of her own book, *Responding to the Call of Ministry: A Study Guide and Workbook for Ministers in Training*. In the course of her work, Rev. Dise has rightly acknowledged the prominence of the National Association of the Church of God in equipping African American women for ministry.

The National Association of the Church of God, headquartered in West Middlesex, Pennsylvania, continues to provide a center for preparation, opportunity, and mentoring for the African American clergywoman. In 1987, a women's convention was birthed as a vehicle to provide opportunities for women to preach on a national level. Evelyn Brown Small served as the president of the National

Association Women of the Church of God when this inaugural event convened in Columbus, Ohio. The conventions continue today as forums for equipping and collaboration.

Clergywomen and those with a heart for ministry continue to lead the National Association Women of the Church of God (NAWCG). Rev. Carol Warner Ligons is the current president of the NAWCG. In 2001 the NAWCG joined with the Women of the Church of God in Nashville, Tennessee, for the Victory–Venture Convention "Woven Together." The two groups convened again in Dallas, Texas, in 2005. Both events were memorable occasions with women from both ministries expressing a desire for future joint conventions.

While the National Association has provided great opportunities for women in ministry, the expansion of roles for African American clergywomen in the national agencies began in the 1980s. African American women are represented in full-time agency posts and continue to serve on national boards. This list of African American women and the posts in which they have served includes and expands on those referenced in Dr. James Earl Massey's book *African Americans and the Church of God*:

1980. Carolyn Waddy Reid, Director of Special Services for Minority Students at Anderson College

1980. Evelyn Wilson, commissioned with her husband, Charles, as missionaries to Kenya, East Africa

1985. Portia Smith Mann, Assistant Director of Security Services at Anderson College; later worked in the admissions office recruiting black students

1988. Mary Woods Baker, Program Coordinator for Women of the Church of God

1988. Jean Morehead, Director of Minority and International Student Services Anderson College

1993. Velma Champlain, Advisor of Multicultural Student Affairs at Anderson University

1999. Cynthia James, Church of God Ministries Council/ Executive Committee

2000. Linda Dowden, Women of the Church of God Board of Directors

2000. Hazel Peters Clark, Women of the Church of God Board of Directors

2001. Sarah Palmer, *ex officio* member of the Church of God Ministries Council

2002. Arnetta McNeese Bailey, joined the staff of Women of the Church of God; became the first African American elected as Executive Director in 2007

2003. Carol Smith, Church of God Bylaws Committee

2003. Annie Ayers, Recording Secretary General Assembly

2003. Saundra McNeese, Women of the Church of God Board of Directors

2004. Diana Lynn Cook Swoope, Anderson University Trustee

2004. Tina Cotto, Business and Leadership Resource Committee

2004. Verda Beach, Anderson University Trustee

2006. Carron Odokara, Church of God Ministries Council

2007. Cynthia James, Special Advisor to the General Director of the Church of God

2007. Deanna Corbett, joined the staff of Women of the Church of God

2008. Suzanne Haley, Chairperson for the Leadership Development Task Force

2008. Carol Merritt, Warner Press Board of Directors

2009. Claretha Free, Christian Women Connection Board of Directors

Although space does not allow us to tell each woman's story, the stories and names included in this chapter are representative of the contributions each woman has made to the Church of God. These women have taken the banner and the message of this reformation movement beyond what our ancestors could have imagined. They have upheld the standards of holiness and unity in the Body and have not been ashamed to join ministry with academia, corporate associations, and community activism. They serve with excellence and are known to expect excellence from those who labor with them.

Rev. Mary Woods Baker

Rev. Mary Woods Baker accepted her call to ministry after an elderly pastor and dear family friend confirmed her feelings. Rev. Baker says, "Since my call to ministry God has allowed me to be promoted to positions that paved the way for and opened doors for other women of color, I praise God for the privilege and honor of being used and also humbled that he has called me to participate in kingdom work."[2]

Rev. Baker was born and reared in Saline, Michigan, the daughter of Paul and Mary Woods. She and her sisters traveled and sang in churches, state conventions, and presented concerts in the United States and Canada. Mary attended Eastern Michigan University and received an associate degree and a bachelor degree from Anderson University. She married Rev. Theodore Baker. Mary said of Ted's passing, "It was a horrific experience, but God gifted me a sense of empathy and compassion as a result of this loss."

As an African American woman, Mary experienced several firsts in ministry. She was the first woman of color to serve in the role of ministry coordinator at Women of the Church of God (now Christian Women Connection). She was also the first African American woman invited to serve on the Madison County Sheriff's Merit Board.

Mary represented Women of the Church of God in Kenya, East Africa; London and Birmingham, England; Sydney, Australia; and Antigua, British West Indies. While attending the World Conference in Nairobi, she was asked to sing in one of the evening services. She sang "There Is a Balm in Gilead." Rev. Baker would later recall that her selection was an expression of her heart: "If you

---

2. Quotes from the women profiled in this chapter from interviews conducted by the author.

cannot preach like Peter, if you cannot pray like Paul, you can tell the love of Jesus; he died to save us all."

The women in the gatherings in which Rev. Baker served were predominantly white. However, Mary found the audience open and receptive and often expressed their appreciation with a small gift. Of those years of service Mary said, "The road has not been easy and oftentimes challenging beyond my strength. I firmly believe God uses our experiences, however difficult, to empower us to better serve to his glory."

Rev. Baker's life exemplifies prayer and humility. Her tenure with Women of the Church of God opened the door for ministry in several feeding programs. In addition, she is currently serving as minister of pastoral care at Sherman Street Church of God and as chaplain in residence at the Anderson University School of Theology.

Mary says, "I am grateful for the men and women who encouraged me in the faith and in my calling. My parents, Sister Ruth Simpson, Rev. Doris Dale, Rev. Ann Smith, Dr. James Earl Massey, Dr. Hollis Pistole, Rev. Jethro Mosley, and Dr. Leroy Quashie. I stand on their shoulders and I reach for the potential that God has for my life. I have not arrived, but like Paul, 'I press towards the goal that awaits me.'"

Rev. Dr. Cynthia Rembert James

"Put away your measuring stick, do not limit God," says Dr. Cynthia Rembert James, daughter of the Church of God reformation movement. Rev. James has received international attention beyond the Church of God for her preaching, teaching, and ecumenical affiliations. She has pastored two congregations simultaneously in Oakland, California, for more than twenty years. Dr. James is the first woman to serve as state pastor in the Church of God. She provides oversight for credentialing, counseling, and pastoral care for approximately 140 pastors and 60 congregations in northern California, northern Nevada, Hawaii, and Guam.

Rev. James has been described as having "a transparent devoutness, coupled with a glaring scholarship." Dr. James has earned two doctoral degrees, one in psychology from Rutgers University, and a doctor of ministry from United Theological Seminary in Dayton, Ohio. Additionally, she was awarded an honorary doctor of divinity degree from Southern California School of Ministry.

Cynthia's counsel and teaching are sought-after commodities. She served as special advisor to Dr. Ron Duncan, general director of Church of God Ministries, until 2012. However, her ministry has taken her beyond the Church of God. T. D. Jakes, founder and pastor of the Potter's House and Woman, Thou Art Loosed Conferences, as well as The Pastors and Leadership Conference, tapped into the ministry of Cynthia and has said of her, "Dr. Cynthia James is in a class all by herself."

Dr. James was consecrated to the office of bishop and serves as the presiding elder of the United Covenant Fellowship, a newly formed collaborative body of approximately ten independent churches and ministries, for diligent and exemplary service to these districts and to the church at large. In 2002, Bishop Cynthia James became the first female bishop elected to the Board of Bishops for the Joint College of African American Pentecostal Bishops' Congress.

Asked once how she would define today's woman, particularly from a spiritual context, and how the message has shifted for today's woman from our mothers' and grandmothers' eras, she commented, "Well, there is biblical foundation for that question. Scripture says, 'Greater work than these shall ye do.' So I think there's a suggestion in that text that while yes, the gospel, the good news, is unchanging, the momentum for it should be increasing. In my own life, that was my mother's message. That message being, 'Don't prepare to serve just one segment; prepare to serve humanity.' That was her message to me from elementary school on."

Rev. Dr. Diana Lynn Cook Swoope

Rev. Diana Lynn Cook Swoope is a wife, mother, proud grandmother, prolific preacher, teacher, visionary, and author. Rev. Diana can also be described as a trailblazer. *Chosen and Highly Favored: A Woman's Sacred Call to Holiness* is the title of one book written by Rev. Swoope; it is, however, also a title that describes who she is. Diana is a woman with a clear call on her life. She had thoughts of becoming a medical doctor, but the call to ministry was louder than the call to medicine.

Pastor Diana is a native of Detroit, Michigan, and the daughter of Rev. Willie James and Elizabeth Johnson Cook. Education has always been paramount in the life of this servant. She received a bachelor of science degree in biology and chemistry from Memphis State University, a master of religious education from Anderson University School of Theology, and a doctor of ministry from Ashland Theological Seminary, where she also served as an adjunct professor in youth ministries. She was awarded an honorary doctor of theology from Asbury Theological Seminary in 2008.

After Diana graduated from Anderson University School of Theology in 1981, Pastor Ronald Fowler invited her to join the Arlington Church of God internship program in Akron, Ohio. In September of that year, she was hired as full-time minister of Christian education and youth.

As a visionary, Diana has chosen not to focus on the lack of opportunities in the church, but has set her sights and dreams on the increased opportunities in the local church for women of all colors. She is the impetus behind the creation of several programs for her church and community. She was instrumental in implementing the EVE Program, a rite-of-passage course for young ladies ages nine to sixteen. She founded the Summer Educational Employment Program, which has helped hundreds of youth to secure summer employment in Akron-area businesses for more than fifteen years.

In 1988 Rev. Dr. Swoope co-founded the Arlington Christian Academy, a chartered elementary school that enrolls students from kindergarten through the eighth grade. Students from this academy have excelled in honors and advanced placement classes in high school and have earned academic scholarships to college.

As a trailblazer, in 1990, Pastor Swoope was the first woman elected as president of the National Inspirational Youth Convention of the Church of God, which began in 1938. In 2009 Rev. Swoope became the first female senior pastor of the Arlington Church of God, after having served the church for twenty-seven years. Of this new assignment Pastor Diana says,

> Perhaps the most significant benchmark that I have experienced in ministry is successfully succeeding a very popular and profitable pastor. When I succeeded the Reverend Dr. Ronald J. Fowler, the church was entering its ninety-first year. It was growing in every way under Pastor Fowler's leadership. In every pastoral transition, there is always concern that momentum will be lost as well as membership. That concern was particularly heightened for some because a female, albeit one who had served the church for 27 years as associate pastor, had been chosen as the next leader. However, much to the delight of most and to the full glory of God, the concerns were obliterated. Indeed, after four years, the church is still growing in every way. It is the Lord's doing, and it is truly marvelous!

The church has frequently called on Rev. Swoope to serve as speaker for conventions, revivals, and seminars all across the United States, Canada, Jamaica, Grand Cayman, Bermuda, Australia, and South Africa.

Rev. Swoope is the author of several books, including *Shout Jubilee! 50 Years of Touching the Lives of Youth* (NIYC Publications, 1990), *Jesus Our Source* (Warner Press, 1997), and *Chosen and Highly Favored: A Woman's Sacred Call To Holiness* (Beacon Hill Press, 2001). She is also a contributing author to several other books.

When asked what life lessons she would share with other clergywomen, Pastor Swoope replied, "Do not argue with a fool because a bystander will not know the difference. I made a decision at the beginning of my public ministry to never argue with those who dispute the biblical call of females to leadership in ministry. My mantra is and always will be, 'I can show you better than I can tell you.'"

Rev. Cynthia Thomas

Ask anyone who has ever been in the company of Rev. Cynthia Thomas whether they have heard her mission statement ("To remain a yielded vessel through which the love and ministry of Jesus Christ may flow at all times, in all circumstances, and to all persons") at least once, and chances are the response will be yes.

Sister Cynthia was born in Decatur, Illinois, the ninth child to John and Christine Hawkins. She had a love for music as a child and showed early signs of leadership at the age of eleven by serving as a substitute Sunday school teacher. The two women role models in her life were her mother, the late Pastor Christine Hawkins, and her sister, the late Johnnie Mae Brown.

Cynthia has been described as "the people's friend." Every facet of her life, whether in the pulpit or in the classroom, has been a place of ministry. Rev. Thomas taught French in the public schools for more than thirty-five years, and her students still refer to her as Madame Thomas. She served as staff developer in the schools and was often found on her lunch hour providing pastoral counseling to teachers, students, and parents.

Always the yielded vessel, she served in several capacities at First Church of God Christian Life Center, Evanston, Illinois. Because she was always willing to lend support, Pastor Thomas was sent by Illinois Church of God Ministries to mentor and assist the new church planters at Agape Christian Fellowship, Round Lake, Illinois, during the years 2000 to 2003.

Women's ministry has always been very important to Rev. Thomas. From 2004 to 2009 she served as the president of the National Association Women of the Church of God. A sought-after conference speaker and gifted preacher, Cynthia's gifts have been used across the country for revivals and special celebrations.

Rev. Thomas serves on the board of Women in Ministry International, an organization for women ministers, whose visionary founder is Dr. Suzan Johnson Cook. Cynthia has served as their representative to the White House and participated in various White House conference calls that addressed social concerns to be clarified for the communities.

When asked about the lessons she has learned along the way, Cynthia replied, "It is just as important to minister to one person as it is to minister to a large group or crowd. Treat every opportunity to minister with energy, patience, and the love of Christ towards those to whom you are ministering."

In 2003, Rev. Thomas was called to serve on the pastoral staff at Langley Avenue Church of God in Chicago, Illinois, where Dr. Noah and Dr. Carolyn Waddy Reid served as pastors. After the Reids' retirement, Cynthia served as interim pastor until the church voted unanimously in October 2012 to make her the senior pastor.

Rev. Dr. Rita Johnson

"Charismatic leadership" is one way to describe the ministry of Dr. Rita Johnson. She was called into the preaching ministry at the early age of sixteen. Her pastor, the late Raymond S. Jackson, called the congregation to a time of fasting and prayer to discover God's purpose and plan for their lives. Dr. Johnson says, "It was during that period of time God led me to Jeremiah 1 and I sensed what others had noticed in me as a child." Rita Joyce Johnson was born in Birmingham, Alabama, and moved to Detroit, Michigan, with her grandparents while she was still an infant.

Dr. Johnson is a graduate of William Tyndale College, with a degree in religious studies, and of Spring Arbor College, with a degree in human resources. She was honored with a doctor of divinity degree by the Southern California School of Ministry.

Always one to move when the Spirit says move, Dr. Johnson is the founder and overseer of Antioch Restoration Ministries

International (ARMI), a network of apostles, prophets, evangelists, pastors, teachers, churches, and parachurch ministries. It has always been Rev. Dr. Johnson's desire to share in ministry across denominational, racial, cultural, and gender lines. Rev. Dr. Johnson is in demand as an apostle, revivalist, workshop, conference, and seminar leader. She has had numerous opportunities to speak at both the North American Convention of the Church of God and the National Association of the Church of God Annual Camp Meeting in West Middlesex, Pennsylvania. Dr. Johnson continues to travel across the world and across denominational and racial lines to declare the message of unity, fellowship, and reconciliation that God has entrusted to her.

Pastor Rita has spent more than forty-five years proclaiming the gospel. On May 6, 2012, after thirty years of pastoral leadership, Rev. Dr. Rita Johnson retired from the pastoral ministry of POWER Centre Church International (formerly Sumpter Community Church of God) in Belleville, Michigan.

When asked what she would share with other clergywomen, Dr. Johnson says, "Too often some women in ministry tend to come across overly aggressive in their attempt to be assertive. There's a big difference between aggressiveness and assertiveness. I have learned to let your life speak for you. Don't take it upon yourself to promote yourself. Let God do it. Practice humility and servanthood. Pattern your life after Jesus and just be the best *you*, because *you* are an original."

Rev. Dr. Kimberly Thomas

Dr. Kimberly Thomas is a woman called to ministry in higher education. She currently serves as an associate professor, teaching classes in specialized ministries, and as senior director of Academics for Spiritual Formation at Mid-America Christian University in Oklahoma City, Oklahoma. Dr. Thomas is also dean of the School of Ministry for the Southern Interstate Ministries Conference of the Church of God. She holds a master's degree in psychology from Texas Southern University and a doctor of ministry from the Houston Graduate School of Theology.

Kimberly Thomas came into this world with a very uncertain beginning. She was born to a woman who, at the time of Kimberly's birth, was living in a physically and emotionally abusive marriage. Seven months after Kimberly was born, a long-term friend of the family, Joan Hill Carter, called her friend, Kimberly's birth mother, to ask if she could come by to give her a break and keep the baby for a few days. A few days of keeping the baby stretched into years of loving care.

Kimberly's family attended the First Church of God in Columbus, Ohio. They later moved to Memphis, Tennessee, where they attended Resurrection Church of God. Having experienced God at young age, Kimberly organized a Youth for Christ group at age fifteen. In her senior year of high school, while attending a National Inspirational Youth Convention, she learned about Gulf Coast Bible College located in Houston, Texas. During Kimberly's years at college, she met and formed lifelong friendships with three women in ministry—Rev. Dr. Doris Ervin, Rev. Dr. Nila Tolliver, and Rev. Evelyn Davis—who influenced her tremendously.

A year after graduating from college, Kimberly married Curtis Thomas. In 1988, Kimberly worked towards a master's degree in psychology. After graduation, she worked for eleven years as an associate school psychologist in the public school district. Her work in the church included teaching Sunday school, chairing the board of Christian education, and directing the church choir, but deep down, she felt there was something more the Lord was calling her to do. In response to the prompting of the Holy Spirit, Kimberly said yes to the call to preach the gospel.

In order to be better equipped for the work of ministry, Kimberly decided to pursue a doctor of ministry degree. Her doctoral dissertation was based on work she did in facilitating a women's support group which explored spiritual healing of emotional trauma from difficult life events. In 1998, she was invited by Dr. Verda Beach, president of Bay Ridge Christian College, to serve as vice president of academic affairs. She learned from Dr. Beach's leadership that a woman in ministry cannot lead with timidity but must courageously lead out as a "Deborah" when called to do so.

In January 2000, Kimberly made a visit to Oklahoma City, and while there she was introduced to Rev. Dr. John Fozard, president of Mid-America Christian University (MACU), formerly Gulf-Coast Bible College. In the course of the conversation, he invited her to consider teaching at MACU. After much prayer and encouragement from her husband, Kimberly followed her dream of teaching at her alma mater. In the fall of 2000, she began her academic ministry career as assistant professor of specialized ministries at MACU.

Kimberly has a passion for married women and for empowering women who are working through traumatic life events. Her ministry audience includes diverse groups of people. She has been guest preacher, teacher, and presenter on church platforms in several states and in Jamaica. She continues to be inspired to develop academic programming in higher education.

Kimberly's ministry journey has taught her the value of mentors in ministry. Her advice to women in ministry is, "Find mentors of women in ministry who are strong, credible, trustworthy, and who will love you. Sit at their feet. Sit at their feet and listen to their stories, listen to their wisdom, listen to their triumphs and failures, listen to their vulnerabilities, listen to their strengths, and ask them hard questions. Ask them the hard questions that you need to know for your own ministry."

Rev. Terri Y. Montague

Rev. Terri Y. Montague ministers bivocationally in the faith community and in the marketplace. She earned her bachelor's degree in economics from the University of Chicago, and dual master's degrees in city planning and in real estate development from the Massachusetts Institute of Technology (MIT). She has attained formal seminary training at Gordon-Conwell Theological Seminary in tandem with her joint studies in law and ethics at Emory University's School of Law and Candler School of Theology.

Rev. Montague says, "I have been blessed to serve in a variety of high-impact leadership roles—often as the first female, African American young(er) person—in both sacred and secular settings. In the Church of God, in particular, I have found a surprising openness to my giftedness." On the national level, she has held office on the Business and Leadership Resource Committee and the Vision-2-Grow Leadership Development Task Force.

From 1990 to 2001 in Boston, Massachusetts, Rev. Montague served on the pastoral team of Shawmut Community Church, where she primarily engaged in discipleship, preaching, and prison outreach ministries. Concurrently, during 1998 to 2000, Rev. Montague chaired the ministerial assembly and served on the credentials committee for the six-state Northeast District of the Church of God. She subsequently was appointed as the district's first area administrator. In these roles, Rev. Montague facilitated district-wide leadership development, administrative and program initiatives, and provided pulpit coverage and other support to local pastors and churches.

Upon relocating to Maryland in 2001, Rev. Montague affiliated with the Monroe Street Church of God, where she functioned as an associate minister while fulfilling an appointment to the Chesapeake-Delaware-Potomac District's Credentials Committee.

Rev. Montague has not only served in ministry but has been a successful voice in the marketplace. She has performed with distinction in global real estate and investments and strategic business operations. From 2001 to 2006, Rev. Montague was called to serve as the national president and chief operating officer at Enterprise Community Partners (formerly The Enterprise Foundation), a leading national provider of capital and expertise for affordable housing and community development. She delivered testimony and presentations to the U.S. House of Representatives Committee on Financial Services, The White House Conference on Minority Homeownership, and a host of other national and regional housing and community development conferences and events. From 2010 to 2012, Rev. Montague applied her passion for thriving and sustainable communities through independent consulting as a part-time Sustainability Fellow, sponsored by Emory University's Center for Community Partnerships. This fellowship focused on planning and developing a pilot program and community partnerships that provided sustainability-related engaged service, learning, and leadership opportunities for Emory students and faculty.

When asked what insights she could share with other clergywomen, Rev. Montague said, "Hone your leadership insights and readiness through professional development in the workplace and through community and board service, if those opportunities are available to you. Keep learning and growing in the grace and knowledge of the Lord, yourself, others, and God's magnificent world—and obtain formal credentials to the extent possible, and in disciplines that complement your ministry calling. Be open and alert to diverse mentors and spiritual advisors—God often sends them in unexpected ways and places."

Presently Rev Montague resides in Atlanta, Georgia, and serves as associate minister at Martin Street Church of God. Her life truly demonstrates the importance of ministry intersecting the marketplace and making a difference for the kingdom.

Rev. Dr. Carol Flewellen Merritt

Wives and husbands serving alongside each other as copastors are becoming prevalent in the African American community as more and more gifted women are recognized as leaders alongside their husbands. Jean and James Morehead pastor Pasadena Heights Church of God in Indianapolis, Indiana; Anita and Antony Parrett pastor Dominion Christian Center in Houston, Texas; Libby and Erwin Lee pastor Morgan Park Church of God in Chicago, Illinois; Donna and Ferrell Roddy pastor Edgemont Church of God in East St. Louis, Illinois; Rochelle and Jeffrey Robinson pastor Total Renewal Church of God in Rex, Georgia. Each of these couples has modeled true partnership on the highest level. Yet, each woman has distinguished herself in her own right, just as Priscilla did in ministry with her husband Aquila.

Dr. Carol Flewellen Merritt and her husband, Pastor Miki Merritt, serve together in ministry at the New Cote Brilliante Church of God in St. Louis, Missouri. They exemplify team ministry at its best. Carol served for ten years in various ministry roles, including minister of music, worship leader, and Christian education before assuming the role of copastor. After Carol accepted her call to ministry, she sensed her role evolving from assisting in ministry to sharing the pastoral call. This new role lends itself to the marriage bond of being "one flesh," and Carole and Miki now cast vision, dream, and plan ministry together. Carol says of being a copastor, "There is no competition, no envy or jealousy, no feeling of being second place. My husband is still my pastor, he is my covering and I am submitted to his leadership and ministry."

African American women are faced with the same challenges that confront all of society. In this ever-changing culture, family, health, and financial stability are universally important components for a quality of life. Abuse on any level, moral decay, a failing educational system, and a failure to recognize equality for all humankind are not issues that affect only one group, but all of society. The faith community has been called to action and African American clergy women in the Church of God have responded to that "Macedonian call" (Acts 13). They recognize that it is not the sole responsibility of the government to address these concerns so they have become educators for a cause. These women have moved forward, understanding that education and empowerment of women are the doors to opportunities. History has proven that education of women has a lasting impact on the family and across generations.

Dr. Cheryl J. Sanders is professor of Christian ethics at Howard University School of Divinity and serves as senior pastor of Third Street Church of God in Washington, DC. In her book *Ministry at the Margins: The Prophetic Mission of Women, Youth and* the Poor, she writes, "Ministry is service that meets needs. This is not a gospel of convenience, but one of sacrifice. Nor is it a gospel of prosperity, you don't serve in order to prosper, you prosper as you serve."[3] Countless women have answered the call to serve and educate through nontraditional ministries and philanthropic endeavors. African American women in the Church of God have designed ministries to heal the hearts of hurting women, ministries that empower our youth, and publishing companies that provide assistance to those with a story to tell. Below is just a sampling of their efforts:

BEaUtiful Girl Empowerment—Tatum Osbourne
When Home Is Not Safe—Zuline Gray Wilkinson
Living Water World Ministry—Jacquie Sharif
Sistah-2-Sistah, If These Walls Could Talk—Dawn Walker
Ministry for Healing Inner Hurts—Pam Gilkes
Metamorphosis Ministries—Felecia Pearson Smith
Priscilla's Lost and Found/Women in Transition—Rev. Arnetta
    McNeese Bailey
Ministry Arts—Elsa Johnson Bass
C.O.M.E. (College Online Ministry Empowerment)—Jewel
    Williams
Write the Vision Independent Publishers—Patrice Turner
Youth Excellence Performing Arts Workshop (YEPAW)—
    Leslie Parker Barnes

We live in a technological age, which gives us an opportunity to witness the dynamic preaching of a new generation. The new generation of African American preachers and teachers are young women who are comfortable with their femininity and their unique styles as women. There is a fresh wind of young women preachers who are teaching the truth and preaching life-changing messages. They are not only speakers but also leaders of cutting-edge ministries that are reaching outside church walls. Tatum Osbourne,

---

3. Sanders, *Ministry at the Margins*, 29.

of New York; Nichole Rawlings, of Chicago, Illinois; and Melanie Thigpen, of Anderson, Indiana, are changing their communities for Christ. When we witness their profound, transforming messages presented with such skill under the anointing of God, we know our future is bright.

The array of gifts among African American clergywomen is vast and the sisterhood that has developed among those in ministry is unshakable. Friendships have been cultivated that echo the nurturing relationship of Mary and Elizabeth. In the words of Patrice Turner, pastor of Grace Place in Chicago, Illinois, these women are "leaping friends," those who celebrate with and encourage one another. African American women have banded together when others have forsaken them and have stood together in one accord, as Mary Magdalene and the other women did at Jesus' tomb. They have dared to answer their unique calling with a universal message of hope: "I have seen the Lord."

The strong foundations of ministry established by gifted African American women in the Church of God continue to make a difference in the movement. These called and gifted women are serving the kingdom in both traditional and innovative pastoral roles. The ministries organized and administrated by these women are vital to the Church of God. May we remember and honor those women who have gone before us, celebrate and be inspired by those women who serve alongside us, and encourage and support those women who will serve after us.

About the Author

Arnetta McNeese Bailey is an ordained minister in the Church of God. She holds a degree in African American religious studies from Ashland Theological Seminary and a master of theological studies degree from Anderson University School of Theology. She is an associate minister of Sherman Street Church of God, Anderson, Indiana.

Arnetta has served Christian Women Connection (formerly Women of the Church of God) since 2002, first as ministry coordinator and now as executive director. Under her leadership, Women of the Church of God conducted the Relevance Study that served as the basis for the transformation into Christian Women Connection to become "a place for every woman, where every woman takes her place." Arnetta is the first African American in the eighty-year history of the organization to serve in this position.

She has also served the National Association of the Women of the Church of God, West Middlesex, Pennsylvania, as stewardship coordinator and vice president. Arnetta is the founder and executive director of Priscilla's Lost and Found and In the Company of Good Men, a faith-based mentoring program for persons in transition.

Arnetta has served extensively as a keynote speaker for national conferences and conventions throughout the United States. In addition to being a featured guest on the Trinity Broadcasting Network, she has preached and taught internationally in the countries of Zambia, Kenya, Uganda, Bermuda, and the Caribbean.

Rev. Arnetta McNeese Bailey and her family are members of the Sherman Street Church of God in Anderson, Indiana. She has three children—Merlelynn, Markus, and Jamal—and is the proud grandmother of two.

CHAPTER 6

Hispanic Women in Ministry in the Church of God

BY NILAH MEIER-YOUNGMAN AND CINDY MANSFIELD

Through the ages, women have responded to Jesus' call to share the liberating gospel even when the faith community did not support them. Hispanic women, like their non-Hispanic sisters, have often lacked affirmation when entering the ministry. Men, by and large, have held the key positions of leadership in Latin America and in the Hispanic Church of God in North America. There have been outstanding pioneering women, however, who have forged a future for other women to follow. I (Nilah) recall how amazed I was, as a girl of twelve, when I heard the news that a woman minister was coming to Argentina from Germany. Her name was Mina Finkbeiner. This single woman preached, held revivals, taught, and did all the tasks of ministry that men did, and she made a deep impression on me.

At the age of seventeen, I was surprised to discover that my own mother had been ordained in 1929 when she completed her training at the Anderson Bible Training School in Anderson, Indiana. All those years she and Father had worked as the first Church of God missionaries from the United States in Brazil and Argentina, and this "secret" had never leaked out! Nobody had asked, I suppose, and Mother, aware of the male dominance in the church in South America, had never shared this fascinating fact. Officially recognized or not, Mother's zeal and passion for her Lord never diminished in forty-two years of service in South America. Side by side with my father, David Meier, my mother, Lillian Meier, evangelized, visited new colonies, cared for nineteen orphans, taught hundreds of children, organized youth and women's groups, prayed for the sick, and proclaimed the Savior everywhere she went.

Today, Tabita Meier Kurrle, Lillian's youngest daughter, carries on her work of missions and ministry in the neighboring country of Paraguay. Tabita and her husband Martin direct a primary school and pastor three congregations.

It would be an impossible task to properly recognize all the outstanding Latina Church of God clergywomen. This chapter seeks to highlight just a few stories from history and ministry today in the twenty-first century.

Ministry Outside the United States

Panama

The year 1988 marked seventy-five years for the Church of God (Iglesia de Dios) in Panama. Two women have played significant leadership roles in the life of the church there: Edith Peters and Daisy Taylor. Reminiscing about how she came to Christ, Peters says, "About forty-seven years ago, on a carnival night, when many of my friends went dancing, I chose to go to church. That very same night the Lord came into my life."

Violet Brewster, wife of a Church of God pastor, influenced young Edith greatly, encouraging her to serve and take active positions in the church. Edith served on the ministerial council, in missionary societies, and as a teacher for more than forty years. For six years, from 1980 to 1986, she served as pastor of the Villa Guadalupe Church. Rev. Edith Peters served as president of the ministerial committee of Panama and was that country's delegate to the Inter-American Conference in Santo Domingo in January 1988. While there, she preached the closing sermon for the newly dedicated Church of God in the Dominican Republic.

Daisy Taylor also grew up in Panama. The model life of her Christian mother guided her early years. In her youth, church services were only in English, and young Daisy felt the Holy Spirit burdening her to share the gospel with her Spanish neighbors and compatriots. She shared her concern with the governing body and they promptly sent her with a witnessing team to begin a mission in Villa Guadalupe. Thus began her ministry, which has continued for more than twenty-six years. Sister Daisy and her husband, Brother Mendoza Taylor, have been outstanding pioneers of the Church of God in Colombia, as missionaries from Panama (and the United States) to that country.

Puerto Rico

Claudina Ocasio de Rivas found the Lord when she was healed from an incurable illness. She has been a pastor in Tomas de Castro, the church she founded in 1973 after a deep burden to share the Lord with the youth and children of her pueblo led her into ministry. Her first years were full of hardship and crisis because others did not want to accept her ministry. "But with much prayer and much love I overcame the obstacles," says Sister "Callita," as she is affectionately called by her children, friends, and parishioners. In Tomas de Castro, this woman reflects God's radiance and compassion. From Tomas de Castro, the ministry has spread to the city of Caguas, where Mary Ann Garcia and her husband Marcos pastor the Ministerios Iglesia de Dios.[1]

Cuba

Carmen Martinez Romero writes, "I met the Lord when I was seven, in a little country church. I dreamed of being a missionary. I

---

1. Quotes from the women profiled in this chapter from interviews conducted by one of the authors.

began preaching at seventeen and have done so ever since…I hope to continue in the Lord's work until God calls me home where I will see God face to face and express my thanks and praises." Rev. Romero has served as president of the National Assembly of the Church of God in Havana, Cuba; has pastored congregations in Cascorro and Marianao; and has been a school teacher and done extensive literacy work in Cuba. She has continued her training in various seminaries.

Recalling her greatest joys, Rev. Romero cites the conversion of her three sons and her youngest daughter's call to ministry. Commenting on how she has been accepted, Hermana (Sister) Carmen says, "My brothers have had to accept my call because they realize it is of God. I did not seek it myself. I say to them, 'If you're unhappy with women in ministry, complain to God. God called me.'" She further explains, "Now in Cuba, women are recognized as equal to men, and they will just have to get used to this new order." This confident leader relies on the Lord to bring about a great revival in Cuba and to keep the churches dynamic and vibrant in their faith.

Mexico

The best-known Hispanic woman leader in Mexico is, no doubt, Amelia Valdez Vazquez. In June 1988, Anderson School of Theology bestowed on Sister Amelia its Distinguished Alumni Award. Amelia has served the Church of God in Mexico for more than thirty years. For twenty-six years, she has taught in Saltillo, Mexico, at LaBuena Tierra Bible Institute (IBB). No other Hispanic woman in our history has had such a long and distinguished career as an educator and pastor.

Amelia first came to know Christ through an invitation by Rev. Una Janes to a revival being held by Rev. A. T. Maciel in Corpus Christi in 1945. That same month Rev. L. Y. Janes baptized Amelia, her mother Andrea, and her sister Manuela. Amelia made a commitment to missionary service at a meeting in which Dr. J. Edgar Smith preached a sermon on consecration. Three pioneers, D. W. Patterson, A. T. Maciel, and L. Y. Janes, were later instrumental in her appointment to Mexico. In 1950, Amelia accepted the invitation from the Board of Church Extension and Home Missions to serve in Mexico. For four years, she pastored the congregation in Nueva Leon and Coahuila. In the summer of 1951, she returned to the States and planted the first Hispanic Church of God in Albuquerque, New Mexico.

For the next twenty-six years, Amelia taught at the Bible Institute in Saltillo. For nine years, while teaching she also pastored the congregation of San Antonio de las Alazanas. One of the highlights of her ministry was "seeing this struggling church come out of conflict and send nine young men and women to be trained at La Buena Tierra." Reminiscing about the promising students she taught, she recalls one named Agustin: "He hardly knew how to read or write when he came to school. Now after graduating he has pastored three congregations, one of which he founded. In three years, the newly founded congregation grew from 0 to 150 in membership. It gives me great delight to have had a part in training this young minister and many others." By the time she retired in June 1988, Amelia had served under the Missionary Board for seventeen years.

Amelia is married to Iamuel Vazquez, an active layperson and a great supporter of Amelia's ministry.

Ministry within the United States

Texas

The Hispanic community in Texas has had two distinguished bilingual teachers who have been models of leadership and inspiration to young men and women pastors alike. Annie Tafolla and Sarah Tafolla Gerodetti played significant roles in the Hispanic church movement in its early days. Their father, Mariano Tafolla, was the pioneer founder of the Spanish Church of God in the United States. He began holding revivals along the Medina River in the late 1920s and 1930s. The congregations of San Antonio and Somerset grew out of these efforts.

Annie Tafolla graduated from Anderson College in 1930 and helped her father in all phases of his ministry. Annie was the speaker at the first meeting Brother and Sister Janes held in Corpus Christi. She also served in the 1950s as the first and only woman (to date) editor of *La Trompeta*, the Spanish Church of God publication. When asked why he stayed true to the Church of God during a period of prejudicial treatment by Anglo leaders, a Hispanic pastor replied, "Sister Annie believed in me! That kept me going." Affirmation and loving encouragement from the Tafolla sisters helped many young Hispanic pastors survive the indifference and neglect they felt in the early years of the Spanish church in Texas.

The Corpus Christi church traces its history to Brother L. Y. and Sister Una Janes, who began their ministry there after returning from a missionary assignment in Panama. Evelyn Janes Anderson, reminiscing about those early days, says that her mother Una was the best teacher and greatest influence on her life. Other Hispanic pastors also have fond memories of this saintly woman who encouraged them to enter the ministry.

Sister Janes held children's meetings in her living room. One day the house was packed with children, so she told her daughter Evelyn to take some of the younger children to the dining room and teach them. So Evelyn, knowing all the Bible stories, began at the age of twelve to teach the little ones, and ever since, Sister Evelyn Anderson has been singing, writing, teaching, preaching, and publishing for the Spanish church. Many of her tracts, written in Spanish, Portuguese, and English, are printed at the Christian Triumph Company and mailed each year to national leaders in South and Central America. Sister Anderson also directs a Spanish correspondence course to train and prepare leaders. As a teenager, Evelyn sought God's will for her life; she received Ephesians 4:12 as her confirmation: "to equip his people for works of service, so that the body of Christ may be built up." For many years she did not understand her ministry, but looking back over her life now, she realizes the fulfillment of that verse in her literature ministry. Her lifelong aspiration to be a missionary was suddenly realized in 1984 when she was invited to Peru to help begin the church in Caja de Agua.

The Christian Triumph Church of God is also in Corpus Christi, pastored by Rev. Israel Hernandez. Oliva Rojas is a member of the pastoral staff there. Rev. Rojas feels that God called her to ministry primarily to address the individual and congregational need for fruitful ministry and fellowship in reconciled relationships.

The greatest number of Latinas in ministry in the Church of God are in the state of Texas. Rev. Uramis Lamelas serves the Spanish language fellowship in Dallas in conjunction with the New Life Biblie Fellowship. There are Churches of God in Jourdanton (pastored by Rosita Cardoza) and San Benito (pastored by Alma Guardiola). Rev. Minga Rangel, who ministers in the Church of God in Somerset, Texas, relates that her call to ministry occurred when her brother was brought back to life after a car accident. The renewal of his physical life created a desire in her to bring life to those who are dead spiritually.

Rev. Diana Rodriguez, discussing the ministry at Eagle Pass, Texas, believes the congregation must inspire people on their journey and be active in using their spiritual gifts. This vibrant border town ministry is having an impact on the community of Eagle Pass and over the border into Mexico. It is reaching beyond the barriers of country and ethnicity to share the gospel of Jesus Christ. As Rev. Rodriguez looks to the future, she sees an urgent need for leaders who share the vision to plant new Hispanic churches on both sides of the border.

The ministry of Gilbert and Melba Davila, now based in Austin, has spanned more than thirty years and has shaped two generations of Hispanic church leaders, including all four of their children. Many children and youth they mentored through the years are now ministering in Texas, New Mexico, Arizona, Colorado, and other parts of the world. Melba says, "We must never underestimate God's power to work in the life of his people. We look back and thank God for leading the way." Aggie Villarreal, founder and pastor of the new Iglesia de Dios congregation in Kingsville, Texas, says, "It wasn't until I started serving in various ministries of the church in Corpus that I began to realize that God was preparing me to become a pastor. In 1986, at the Hispanic Church of God Convention, I was assured of my calling." For nine years, Aggie was active in Pastor Gilbert Davila's congregation. He encouraged her to begin the Kingsville work when she shared her burden to start a church in her hometown. John, her husband, supports Aggie's ministry and directs the music. Ana, her seventeen-year-old daughter, teaches Sunday school. Aggie's favorite scripture is Proverbs 3:5–6, "Trust in the LORD with all your heart and lean not on your own understanding; in all your ways submit to him, and he will make your paths straight" (NIV).

Florida

Hilaria and Ellsworth Palmer pastored the Cuban Church of God in Miami for twenty-eight years. The church began in the living room of the Palmer home during the Cuban refugees' flight to Florida in 1960. Each Wednesday morning, women from the church and community gathered to lift up to God the problems and needs of their neighborhood. Sister Hilaria tells incredible stories about the love and power of God experienced in these meetings and the many lives that were transformed and homes changed. This was the beginning of the Spanish-language congregations in Miami. Today, the ministry with Latinos continues: Idalmis Martinez, co-pastoring with her husband Jorge at the Miami Spanish Church of God; and Raquel Grizzell co-pastors with her husband at the Greater Miami Iglesia de Dios. Both of these churches are growing under a model of ministry partnership.

Oregon

Rev. Cati Perez-Scrivner left Texas as a young bride to live with Merle, her husband, in Portland, Oregon. In these new surroundings, Cati discovered that many Mexicans had come to Oregon to pick fruit, and she felt burdened for these migrant workers. She says, "I saw my people with emptiness in their faces and I had a burning ache in my heart to tell them about Jesus. I knew my Savior could fill that emptiness."

Cati recently retired as pastor of the Ministerio Latino in the Rockwood Church of God in Portland, Oregon, a church she pastored for more than twenty years. The congregation has grown to an attendance of 180 people; the church had to purchase a second bus in order to transport more people from the migrant camps! Cati's guiding theme is to bless others, and discipling laypeople is basic to her ministry approach.

New Mexico

Shortly after their marriage, Cindy and Richard Mansfield moved to Corpus Christi, Texas, to work for an insurance company. Their new neighbors, Felix and Sylvia, led them both to the Lord. They soon became involved in the outreach ministries of the Iglesia de Dios pastored by Gilbert Davila. They joined a music group called Blessings and held concerts. Richard guided the prison ministries team, and Cindy played the drums and worked with the drama and youth departments. One night after watching *Fantasy Island*, Cindy asked Richard to tell her his fondest fantasy. Richard replied, "To pastor my very own church!" One month later, they received a call from the Board of Church Extension and Home Missions to become the pastors for the Albuquerque Hispanic Church of God.

They could write books about their experiences with gang violence in the neighborhood and the miracles God has worked in the lives of families and young people. To build self-esteem among the teenagers of the Southside community, Cindy has organized a drum corps. They hope to "lead the parade for Jesus" in their city. Cindy has held leadership positions as Sunday school superintendent and preacher and is the first Hispanic American elected as the national spiritual life director for the Women of the Church of God (now Christian Women Connection). Cindy and Richard feel a deep sense of calling and teamship for ministry and know that Romans 8:28 is true: God does work in all things for good.

Ohio

After hours of prayer one night in October 1982, Tina Cotto made a pledge to God that she would study for the ministry. Pastors Harold and Jackie Harrison were the most influential people in young Tina's walk with Christ. "They were my spiritual godparents...All they said, they lived. That gave me hope. There was also, in them, such a sense of urgency and deep yearning to share Christ. That impressed me," says Tina. Later, when Tina met Sister Hattie Downer in Brooklyn, New York, she was utterly fascinated by this saintly woman's radiance and joy. Sister Hattie, a wise leader, discerned Tina's gifts for ministry and encouraged her to share, preach, and witness in the church.

One summer at a youth camp she met David Cotto. "I fell in love with that man's spirit," she recalls. In September 1982 they were married. "I have been so blessed," says Tina. "David, my beloved husband, encourages my potential. We have two beautiful daughters, and I have come to know that in Christ I am somebody! My whole being blesses God when someone is healed or finds Christ or when a woman understands her self-worth." As pastors of the Hispanic church in Washington, DC, David and Tina stressed making converts into disciples. This remains their focus as pastors of the Clifton Avenue Church of God in Springfield, Ohio.

New York

In 1983 Rosita Dominguez, a young woman from El Salvador, began to hold Bible studies in her New York apartment. Rosita came from Rev. Tito Ayala's church in El Salvador with a great burden to share Christ with the Hispanic community in New York City. She began to work with Sister Hattie Downer in Brooklyn. Today, Rosita's ministry is very promising and she needs our prayers and support as she tries to be a witness for Christ. With over a million Puerto Ricans and Hispanics, New York City is a mission field ripe for the harvest.

A new day is dawning on the Hispanic horizon. In both Americas, women are responding to Christ's call to witness, love, heal, reconcile, bind up wounds, feed the hungry, and proclaim the Light of the World!

About the Authors

Nilah Meier-Youngman is an ordained minister in the Church of God. She has served as director of Hispanic Ministries with the National Board of Church Extension and Home Missions. Nilah has served as a professor at Anderson University, as Director of Hispanic Ministries for the Church of God, and has been a guest lecturer and speaker for more missions conferences and conventions than can be remembered. As of the writing of this second edition, Nilah resides in a skilled nursing facility, where she continues to encourage all those around her.

Cynthia Mansfield is a licensed minister of the Church of God, where her calling is to teach, train, equip, encourage, and mobilize women for leadership. She is also the general manager of KNAT-TV, a full-power affiliate of the Trinity Broadcasting Network. Cindy produces and directs a half-hour public affairs program for TBN, inviting city and state officials to discuss pressing issues and needs in the state she and her husband (Richard) have called home for more than twenty-five years: New Mexico.

As a member of the National Board of Directors for CWC (Christian Women Connection) Cindy serves the Desert/Rocky Mountain Region (Utah, Colorado, Arizona, and New Mexico) and helped initiate a joint venture with Spanish-speaking women within the United States and around the world with the new edition to the CWC website with Spanish resources available for outreach. Cindy is also the liaison to the Hispanic Council of the Church of God: Mujeres de la Iglesia de Dios. New Beginnings Church of God in Albuquerque, New Mexico, is Cindy's church home, where she serves as the director of women's ministry and worship team chaplain.

CHAPTER 7

Women in Cross-Cultural Missions of the Church of God

BY DONDEENA CALDWELL AND KATHI SELLERS

The press clanked as the master printer operated it with her foot. Ruth Murray was turning out Sunday school helps for the Church of God in Kenya, along with devotional materials, school books, song sheets, and eventually a hymnbook of three hundred songs. She often illustrated the materials with hand-drawn pictures.

Gertrude Kramer and Mabel Baker worked closely with Murray in the early 1900s, providing the translated materials for her to print. Kramer also translated the New Testament into the dialect of the Olunyore tribe, often with her children by her side, clamoring for attention. Baker made the spelling uniform and revised Kramer's translation into the more idiomatic language of the tribe, and in 1938 the American Bible Society printed the Kramer-Baker translation of the New Testament.

These women were some of the pioneers in the work of the Church of God in Kenya. Their contributions went beyond denominational boundaries and helped to spread the good news to all of the Olunyore tribe. Their call to follow Christ also went beyond the traditional expectations of marrying a committed Christian man and supporting his ministry through homemaking and raising a family. Kramer, Baker, Murray, and many women before and since have used their spiritual gifts as cross-cultural missionaries. They responded to the call to proclaim the gospel to people of another culture.

The first woman of the Church of God to be part of a cross-cultural mission is remembered only as "Mrs." She and her husband, John Rupert, went from the United States to England in 1892 when the Church of God reformation movement was just twelve years old. Historical records have left her nameless, faceless, and with no acknowledgment of her contribution as a missionary.

By 1911, five more women had accompanied their husbands overseas, yet we have no record of four of these women's names. In more formal times, women were often known only as "Mrs." and the husband's surname. George and Mrs. Martin went to England and Scotland in 1891. In 1904, George and Mary Bailey went to India. In 1908, another George took his name-unknown wife, Mrs. Pye, to Trinidad. In the early years of missionary outreach, inadequate records are understandable; but nineteen and twenty years after the first missionary left the United States border for Mexico, two women were still nameless and faceless, with no record of their cross-cultural contributions. Edward and Mrs. Reedy went to Trinidad in 1911. The following year, Robert and Mrs. Springer went to Russia and Switzerland.

Even after the formal organization of the Missionary Board of the Church of God in 1909, three married women who accompanied their husbands on missionary assignments were nameless: Mrs. Samuel Joiner (Kenya, 1922), Mrs. William Conkis (Egypt, 1933), and Mrs. George Dallas (Egypt, 1933). No men's names seem to have been lost, nor have any names of single women missionaries been forgotten. The lack of acceptance of women as persons in their own right, rather than as extensions of their husbands, remained a problem for many years. One former missionary to Kenya said, "I was looked on by most of the male missionaries as just a wife and young mother. It was frustrating to be considered only a 'missionary's wife.' We both felt called, commissioned, and sent. It seemed unfair that the single females were considered to be missionaries, but we wives were there mainly for support."

That sense of call from God to serve in a cross-cultural setting was expressed in a 1988 survey of former and present missionary women. Out of thirty-six responses, only three indicated that they went overseas solely because of their husband's call. More than half of the women felt called to missions during their youth, some as young as six years of age. Many had parents with a global consciousness. The call came after exposure to missionaries, reading missionary books, or working with women's missionary groups. Others were challenged through student volunteers, Tri-S (Student Summer Service of Anderson University), and religious emphasis weeks on campuses.

Twyla Ludwig felt God's call to go to Africa (Kenya, 1927–49) even before her husband John was converted. No one who has read *Mama Was a Missionary*, written by her son, Charles Ludwig, could doubt that Twyla was a full participant and missionary in her own right. Ruth Shotton, who served in Mexico, Panama, and Venezuela says, "I was uneducated, had a husband who had been a Christian only a few years, and had four children: God made it clear to me my calling, 'The Spirit of the Lord is upon me, because he hath anointed me to preach the gospel'" (Luke 4:18–19).

This strong sense of calling has sent women, both single and married, into many countries of the world with the gospel. Most have been involved in the helping professions, such as nursing, teaching, and social work, where demands and responsibilities correspond to those of a home. Not all women aspire to leadership positions, but many do possess the gifts of administration or preaching. Each of these women must be accepted according to her gifts as translator, teacher, administrator, medical worker, or preacher, not because of her gender but because she is using her spiritual gifts within the authority of the church.

In spite of a lack of encouragement at times, women in the Church of God have made, and continue to make, an invaluable contribution to the church and the world. In fact, the majority of missionaries sent out by the Church of God has been and continues to be female. Well over one hundred single women are part of this great host of cross-cultural missionaries, some serving only one year and others for as long as thirty-nine years (Mabel Baker and Josephine McCrie).

The first single woman to go as a missionary was Lena Shoffner, who went to England in 1893 and worked for two years. Nine more singles followed her example in the following decade, going to Mexico, India, Trinidad, Russia, and Jamaica. Outstanding among them was Josephine McCrie, who spent thirty-nine years in India. Between 1910 and 1920, thirteen single women were called to serve in Denmark, Sweden, China, Syria, Barbados, Trinidad, India, Kenya, and Japan. Among them was Nellie Laughlin, who worked in Syria with F. G. Smith, his wife Birdie, and Bessie Hittle. When World War I erupted, the missionaries found themselves in enemy territory and were advised to leave. The other three left, but Nellie chose to stay. By 1917, all communication with the outside world was cut off. She managed to find enough food to keep herself and a small group of believers alive. "She spent her time training these young converts in biblical truth. Nellie had become a full-time missionary and was the only missionary of the Church of God in that entire area."[1] Following the war, she made the decision to move the work of the church from the small village of Schweifat to the city of Beirut, the kind of decision usually made by male leadership. Nellie later served in Egypt until her retirement.

Mabel Baker arrived in Kenya in 1914 and spent thirty-nine years involved in many aspects of the work there. She became the chairperson and treasurer of the African Assembly while John and

---

1. Crose, *Passport for a Reformation*, 43.

Twyla Ludwig were on furlough. At the same time, she was educational secretary for all the village schools. She managed the bookshop, translating, printing, and supplying Sunday school material for the villages. She was also treasurer for the girls' school. The younger Africans declared that she had a greater Olunyore vocabulary than any of them.[2]

Daisy Maiden Boone and Belle Watson went to China in 1916. They had an evangelistic ministry and shared the gospel at every opportunity. The women helped with church planting and developing church leaders, especially "Bible Women" who traveled to share the Word of God. After twenty-one years of service in China, Belle retired from missionary service. Daisy continued without Belle, leaving China in May 1949 because of the Communist takeover.

In the decade of the 1920s, single women went to Ireland, India, Japan, Kenya, and Jamaica. Among them were Edith Young, who spent thirty-seven years in Jamaica; Naomi Allan, who spent thirty-six years in Ireland; and Mona Moors, who spent thirty-three years in India. Young taught full time at Jamaica Bible Institute until her retirement. Allan's contribution to kingdom work was to edit the British edition of the *Gospel Trumpet*. When Moors first went to India, she was put in charge of a home for boys in Cuttack. Later, she managed a shelter for girls, along with Indian sisters Sonat and Nolini Mundul, giving most of her time to the care and education of the girls. Ellen High joined Mona Moors in Cuttack in 1937 and worked in India for twenty-one years.

Other single women went to Cuba, Kenya, and Egypt during the 1930s. One of these, Lima Lehmer Williams, spent twenty-nine years at the hospital and school in Kima, Kenya. Besides teaching Bible to the women of various villages, she and Jewell Hall taught weekly Bible classes at Mwihila for pastors who had no formal training. *Walking in Missionary Shoes* tells of Lima's missionary experiences.[3]

---

2. Williams, *Walking in Missionary Shoes*, 99.
3. Ibid.

Fourteen single women were sent by the Missionary Board in the 1940s to work in cross-cultural missions. They went to Grand Cayman, Kenya, China, Cuba, Jamaica, Antigua, and St. Kitts. After spending a year in Antigua, Wilhelmina Fraser continued to work with the church in St. Kitts for twenty-eight years. Three women who went to Kenya during that decade remained for more than twenty years: Jewell Hall, Irene Engst, and Lydia Hanson worked for twenty-eight, twenty-seven, and twenty-four years respectively. Their medical and teaching skills brought healing and training to an untold number of people. Jewell Hall opened a teacher training facility in Mwihila. Engst wrote, "I helped get the Mwihila medical work started by holding a dispensary first outdoors and then in a small building. I helped start the women's work in Kenya, taught in the Teacher Training Center, and did general mission work."[4]

For the next two decades (1950–69), the majority of single women involved in Church of God missions went to Kenya as nurses. Vera Martin served as a nurse and taught nursing for fifteen years as the matron of nursing. During her twenty-two-year career in Kenya and Uganda, Cornelia Barnette Kerich served six years as a single nurse beginning in 1967. The three women with the longest tenure in Kenya during this period are Edna Thimes (nineteen years), Velma Schneider (sixteen years), and Vera Martin (fifteen years). Through Thimes's efforts and the practice of preventive medicine, such as vaccination and immunization, the cases of polio and other childhood diseases diminished in the Kima-Mwihila area. Martin was on the Medical Council of Kenya, which included all government and mission hospitals. She sat on the licensing board for four years to review nurses who entered the colony for registration. Because of her contacts, the Church of God in Kenya received many considerations, such as free food for the needy and free medications.

During the history of Church of God missions, 46 percent of all single missionaries have gone to Kenya. About one-third were involved in educational work, one-third in the medical program,

4. Ibid.

and one-third in direct church-related work. The British colonial government provided financial grants to Christian missions involved in education and medical services to help the country develop more rapidly. This gave women with such skills the financial support to serve overseas.

Kenya again headed the list for single missionaries in the 1970s and 1980s. Caroline Ackerman gave thirty-two years to nursing in Kenya and Tanzania, beginning her career in 1970. Her last fifteen years in Tanzania were served in community-based health care. By the early- to mid-1980s, the largest numbers of missionaries ever were sent to Kenya, and most of them were women. Rebecca Pierce went to Kenya in 2000 as the first nurse to serve at Kima International School of Theology (KIST), a position she held for ten years.

Other women used their skills as teachers, for the most part, in Japan, Mexico, Brazil, Hong Kong, and Taiwan. A trend of shorter terms of missionary service emerged. Most who went overseas during the 1970s and 1980s gave three to five years of their lives as teachers or nurses rather than becoming career missionaries. Not everyone is called to be a career missionary, and there are not as many opportunities today for single women to dedicate the rest of their lives in such work. As the national church of each country matures and grows, it finds leadership among its own people, usually among the men. Carroll, Hargrove, and Lummis say,

> Changes in the status and visibility of women in churches have been in response to internal phases within the life cycle of religious movements. Women have usually been permitted freedom of expression and exercise of leadership in the first stage of the movement, or "charismatic phase."
>
> As the movement becomes older and larger, it enters its "consolidation and organization phase" in which women are absorbed into a system dominated by men and not allowed much autonomy of expression, organization, or decision-making.[5]

---

5. Carroll, Hargrove, and Lummis, "Women of the Cloth."

The trend toward shorter terms of missionary service in the last few decades is probably a reflection of the trend in our society. Statistics now show that those who entered the job market in the 1980s expected to change jobs between twelve to fifteen times during their working lives.[6]

The response to a survey in 1988 by Dondeena Caldwell found that most single women missionaries felt equally valued and involved, while more wives than singles had ambivalent feelings about their worth and acceptance. Granted, both married or singles must earn respect from their colleagues, but the way a woman feels about her contribution and self-worth as a missionary often is determined by her personality, training, husband-wife relationship, and the opportunities she is afforded (or not afforded) to use her God-given talents. Another factor that helps to determine whether equal partnership in mission can exist for women is the attitude toward them in the local culture.[7]

"My husband was looked upon as the one having more experience," responded one woman who had worked in Kenya. From Japan a wife wrote, "The national church leaders would probably take my husband's opinion over mine." And from Bolivia, where women are to be observers rather than leaders, Barbara Miller, an ordained minister, says, "I relate well to Bolivian brethren, but I am not considered an equal to my husband when it comes to missionary duties and responsibilities." On the other hand, Ruth Shotton tells about her experiences in Mexico and Panama: "In Mexico I worked undercover or behind the scenes because of *machismo* in the masculine society. In Panama I was more openly accepted, especially by the black culture. This was a carryover from the favorable acceptance of their own women as leaders. On the Kuna Yala Islands, the Kuna Indians have a matriarchal society. Their male leaders sometimes turned to me before they did to my husband."

While women in missions are respected, some feel more acceptance than others. "I am respected," says a missionary from

---

6. Caldwell, "Single Woman's Contribution to Missions."
7. Caldwell, "Missionary? Wife? Or Both?"

Tanzania, "but I am not taken into confidence." "I am the missionary's wife," says another woman, "not the missionary," even though she is a licensed minister. "I was viewed by the men as a girl, an unmarried woman, but fully valued by the women of Kenya," reported another. Many women expressed feeling that the national leaders expected more from them than from their own women. Kay Critser, retired missionary, wrote, "I am viewed by the nationals as a foreigner who has come with expertise which they can use. I have found that when women have proven that they have abilities other than what society has decreed they should have, they are respected by men as long as they in return respect them."

The acceptance of women in positions of leadership has changed over the years. Retha Shultz states, "In Kenya many areas exist, certainly in the home, where the man is 'king.' In the church the men are by far the most prominent. The interesting fact is that men are realizing that the women are the ones with a tremendous ability to manage the affairs of the household and also of the church. Even the government appointed women instead of men to be in charge of some of the programs which had been set up." Jenny Schwieger adds, "Today many women are in leadership roles in the Kenyan church and are listened to and serve on many decision-making committees. The role of the missionary has changed from leader or 'all-knowing one' to advisor and co-worker. The co-worker response to women missionaries has come with the leadership of Marilyn Farag, who always made sure that the decision of the Africans was acted upon rather than her decision."

Most women feel valued if they work within the confines of the cross-cultural situation, which usually means working with women. Such a woman is Frances Clark, who recalls her work in East Pakistan: "I was a full partner with my husband, in charge primarily in the home, with women, children, health and home training—areas impossible for men to enter. I did not feel mine was a second-class role in any sense, nor was I encouraged to feel so." The most frustrating experience, though, is to feel that within our own North American culture, women still are considered to be less than co-workers with their husbands and male colleagues. One former missionary wrote, "The political structure of the church, missions, and government were always kept in male hands. I wrote letters to the executive officers of the Missionary Board and signed my husband's name because I knew they would be dealt with as being of greater significance. I practiced this all fifteen years of our relationship with the board. I felt it was a necessary procedure to reach desired goals." Women want to be accepted as an integral part of the decision-making and work involvement as missionaries. That their responsibilities often are limited to women and children might at first seem to be unjust. However, research shows that most people come to faith in Christ between the ages of four and fourteen, so perhaps the women have actually been give the greatest harvest field.[8] "Don't slight women's ministries," says Mary Lou Walls, former missionary to Venezuela. "That should be an integral part of a woman as missionary. She is the female example and leader."

Because women make up more than half of the world's population, they should be the recipients of at least half of our time and efforts. Who could be more aware and sympathetic of women and their needs than a woman of God who is striving to serve those who suffer injustice and deprivation? As missionaries work with women, they discover those who are dynamic agents for change in our world. Women's "existential link to life fosters attitudes in them that are life preserving and life enhancing…Wherever women engage in processes of self-dignification and join forces with others, they embody courage and hope and become agents for change."[9]

Such change came to the women in the Church of God in Brazil. In 1971, a local pastor announced the annual business meeting would be held at the end of the service. As was the custom in every church, he ended the announcement saying, "All women and children will be excused." Seventy percent of those present filed out without saying a word. That all changed, however, after the women were given a chance to develop their leadership abilities through

---

8. "4/14 Movement." http://4to14window.com. Accessed October 20, 2012.

9. Garcia, "Women's Ministries," 30.

a local and national women's organization. Their efficient business meetings and successful budgetary goals, as well as their increased knowledge of the Bible and missions education, were a challenge to the General Ministerial Assembly. Today the women in the church in Brazil are accepted as valued partners because someone saw value in them and in the "women's work" performed by missionaries.

The church in several countries has been enhanced through the work of organized women's groups, work that brings self-dignification and development to women. Missionaries in Japan, Jamaica, Mexico, Brazil, Venezuela, Kenya, Egypt, the Caribbean, Uganda, and other areas have lifted the hopes and skills of women through the unique contributions of such organizations.

Christian Women Connection (formerly Women of the Church of God) in North America also is deeply involved in cross-cultural mission, supporting projects to relieve hunger, educate, and build necessary facilities around the world. The hospital and first missionary residence at Mwihila were built with funds from Women of the Church of God. They also provided money to build the first church in Mexico City. Many leaders from other countries have received scholarships from the women for advanced training. This indirect cross-cultural assistance strengthens what missionary women do while serving overseas.

Most women feel they are or have been an integral part in decision-making among their missionary colleagues. Edna Thimes, a single missionary to Kenya, reported that she was involved in decision-making in the General Assembly, the Executive Council of the same, the Board of Christian Education, the college and hospital of the Church of God, and the Friends Hospital and Anglican Hospital in the community. The church in Kenya even ordained her.

Ruth Sanderson left Kenya in 1958, two years before Edna Thimes arrived. Sanderson's experience while there reflects only some of the changes that took place after she left. She says, "Missionaries held staff meetings, and I had a vote. However, most of the men were on most of the committees. All of the men were ordained, no matter what their previous occupation or training. None of the women were ordained. They tended to do 'women's work' except in emergencies."

Retha Shultz, who served with her husband in Trinidad, added, "In some areas I was an integral part. However, when it came to the official committees of the church, usually I was not an officer or involved officially." She and others would agree with Roberta Hestenes, who said, "I was encouraged to share my faith actively while always granting to men the formal positions within our church."[10]

Phyllis Kinley, who served in Japan with her husband from 1958 until her retirement in 1999, observes that at the time of her calling to cross-cultural mission women were not challenged to become ordained ministers. Instead, she chose to marry a minister and share in his work. Because her husband Philip was the director of Tamagawa Seigakuin Girls School, she did much of the pastoral work in the Hagiyama Church and much of the actual evangelism and counseling. It was either that or close the church for lack of leadership. If Phyllis Kinley had gone to Japan as an ordained minister, today she would automatically be a member of the Renmei, the Japanese Association of the Church of God, and also be a part of the pastors' decision-making body. "Because I was not ordained," she says, "I could not baptize persons, conduct communion services, or pronounce the benediction. I could do almost anything else, including preaching when my husband was away." (Philip was considered the legal pastor of the church, even though she did most of the work.) Phyllis's inability to perform certain pastoral tasks, or to be a part of the Renmei and pastors' group, stem not so much from her gender as from her lack of ordination. In this case, ordination means authority because the decisions of the church are made by the ordained.

For decades, the married female missionary worked for little or no pay; her role was largely defined by her husband's assignment. She was expected to support and adapt to his vocation, as her husband's work was often seen as the real mission work. Even though

---

10. Hestenes, "Is the Gospel Good News for Women?"

both partners of a missionary couple were considered missionaries, they shared a check, Social Security, retirement, and other benefits. The missionary wife went through the same application process as her husband. They both received field orientation (often considered inadequate), and both were included in the commissioning service. Yet the wife usually had no particular assignment; she had to find her own avenue of service. She was neither required nor pressured to do mission work other than caring for her home and family.[11] Ann Smith says that she knew nothing of cross-cultural skills before going to Japan in 1951. Ruth Kilmer states, "We had no orientation in mission work, methods, or even the history of the station and culture to which we were being sent. Some things we learned the hard way." Given the little direction and even less preparation, the significant contributions women made to the mission of the Church of God are miraculous. Today, married women are employed separately from their husbands and generally have a specific ministry assignment. The couple shares one salary package, but it is frequently divided and in the name of each individual. Most married women are directly involved in mission work and consider themselves members of a team.

Women in cross-cultural situations often find unique ways to meet the needs of the community and the church. For example, several women have used their skills as bookkeepers for schools, hospitals, mission staffs, or assemblies. Margaret Tiesel taught proper bookkeeping methods to church treasurers in the West Indies. Bernie Dean helped to get a business department started at Ardenne High School in Jamaica.

The contribution of women to education, both secular and religious, has no equal. Lester Crose writes about Nellie Olson, who organized not one but two educational institutions: "In 1928, Nellie Olson, feeling the need for a better-trained ministry, opened the Jamaica Bible Institute. She observed immediately that most of the students had not yet completed secondary school, and the very

---

11. Bowers, "Roles of Married Women Missionaries."

next year she opened a high school department at the institute."[12] The new department became Ardenne High School, which to this day remains one of the outstanding secondary schools in Jamaica.

Margaret LaFont served for twenty-seven years in Kenya and founded the Bunyore Girls School, which today is one of the finest girls' schools in the country, with a student body of more than one thousand girls. Nina Ratzlaff started the Triple C School in Grand Cayman, which continues to do well. Later she taught Christian education at the Jamaica Bible Institute. Caroline Armstrong, along with her husband Don, founded the Aldersgate School in Tanzania, a highly acclaimed school that is fully self-supporting. Many other women have been the guiding force to educate children, train teachers, and create or translate curricula and books for use in classrooms and the church.

Women have been involved in planning for and teaching in several other Bible institutes. Retha Shultz helped organize the Bible school in Trinidad; she also taught there. Shultz was later a teacher in two other Bible schools. Mary Butz was the force behind the Bible institute in Peru. Dondeena Caldwell helped to organize, direct, and teach in Bible schools in Mexico and Brazil. Jean McCracken organized and taught theological education by extension throughout Northern Brazil. Mary Ann Hawkins helped to establish Kima International School of Theology (KIST) in Kenya, where she later served as academic dean. Tammie Tregellas taught at KIST and has trained pastors and leaders in Zambia, Malawi, and Mozambique. Kay Critser has been involved in leadership development and was one of the teachers at IBAO (West Africa Bible Institute) in Côte d'Ivoire. Don Deena Johnson served as dean at Mediterranean Bible College in Lebanon and taught extension classes in Egypt. Today Abby Smith teaches pastors and leaders Church of God history and other courses in Colombia.

A number of women were involved in teaching and training leaders. Marion Hoffman is a pioneer missionary who, along with her husband Stan, planted churches in Tanzania, Uganda, and

---

12. Crose, *Passport for a Reformation*, 84.

Zambia. They prepared and trained new converts to pastor and lead the new churches. Marion was known as a great prayer warrior, and many healings and powerful deliverance resulted from her prayers. Over the years many women have served as teachers of conversational English as a means to share the gospel cross-culturally. Susan Hardman gave twenty-one years teaching English in China, sharing Christ's love and grace as she planted the seed of the gospel. Zonia Mitchell spent twenty-two years teaching English at Saga University in Japan, discipling students, and participating in the Saga Church of God. Cheryl Johnson Barton, a missionary kid, lived her adult life as a missionary in Japan teaching, pastoring, and writing.

Another important contribution of women to cross-cultural missions is as music teachers. True, people of every culture sing and play indigenous musical instruments, but often they have no written music, nor could they read it if it were available. Women, more often than men, have taught piano, voice, and music theory to indigenous worship leaders. In Costa Rica, Gloria Plank taught music to the pastors and leaders of the church, while Brenda Maxfield, along with her husband Paul, improved the quality of music in the churches through the children's choir. At the VII World Conference held in 1983 in Nairobi, Kenya, the executive officer of the Church of God, Byrum Makokha, introduced several outstanding choirs from Kenyan churches. He said, "We Africans have always been able to sing. We have a good sense of rhythm, but it took the missionary to teach us how to sing in harmony." Much of the credit can be given to people such as Fern Ludwig Rogers, who organized the annual music festivals of Kenya, and Grace Donohew, who translated and printed *Waves of Devotion*, a hymnbook, into the Luyia language.

In Brazil, music once played only a minor role in the church; sermons provided spiritual validity to church services. After missionary women trained choirs and musicians, however, the Brazilian women asked the all-male ministerial assembly to allow a choir to perform a cantata during the annual convention. One pastor responded, "Do you mean there will be no sermon? How can that be spiritual?" More people came to the altar for prayer after the cantata than after any sermon during the convention! Music is now used as a dynamic witness in the church and to the community.

The work women have done to build communities and equip the church is varied and sometimes surprising. They have drawn plans for dormitories, homes, and a hospital, and then worked side by side with male colleagues to construct the buildings, laying bricks and placing tiles on the roofs. A few, like Tammie Tregellas in Malawi, have even supervised the construction of buildings. Glenna Yutzy's work was unique: She operated a short-wave radio three times a day to other mission stations. Kay Critser reports working with the people in Tanzania to plant an eight-acre field of corn. Sue Joe Good worked in the rice fields with women in Magugu, Tanzania.

Other contributions from women in cross-cultural missions include working with refugees, prostitutes, and the mentally and physically handicapped. Colleen Stevenson has been a tireless advocate for education for children, for AIDS victims, to provide homes for grandmothers, and for entrepreneurial opportunities for women in Uganda. Rhonda Philips ministers to women caught in the sex trade in Europe. Carrie Critser worked in Central Asia with disabled children through music and art therapy.

Women missionaries were, at one time, seldom recognized as executives or thought to be capable of making top-level decisions. A majority of missionary women in Dondeena Caldwell's 1988 survey reported that the church makes little use of their skills and experience when they return home. Said one, "The church does not use my skills in any special way. I am usually asked only the questions that pertain to the women's daily life. The wife and children seem to be on exhibit more than contributing to the mission enterprise." Another added, "It is possible that the American church does not really value the experience and skills of the missionary woman upon her return. Skills of knowledge, insight, culture, and language are often ignored on the part of American society because they are unimportant to them."

Two missionaries gifted in administration were Dorothy Sharp and Magaline Hoops. Sharp was surprised that she was asked, instead of her husband, to be the Kenyan mission's interim secretary-treasurer. Dot's husband, Jim, was supportive of her in that position; from others, however, she got the impression that no major decisions were to be made during her one-year tenure. After the death of Roy Hoops, his wife Magaline became the mission secretary-treasurer for Tanzania, serving in that position for three years. Later she moved to Kenya and was asked in 1988 to become the mission secretary-treasurer there. Because of her position, she was included on several committees with the Kenyan church's national leadership, and occasionally she had trouble among her male colleagues who were unaccustomed to being answerable to a woman.

Ann Smith and Gwendolyn Massey were some of the first women to serve on the administrative staff of the Missionary Board. Sharon Skaggs served with the Missionary Board/Global Missions in a variety of executive positions until her retirement in January 2012. Both Joyce Hazen and Kathi Sellers served as missionaries and then came to the office of Global Missions to serve in recruitment and member care. Jamie Nachtigall works as a full partner with her husband as regional coordinators for Europe and the Middle East. She is fully involved in the administrative role and often is responsible for the administrative tasks. Other regional coordinators, including Caroline Armstrong and Barbara Miller, preach, teach, and are actively involved in the administrative tasks of the role.

Many women in cross-cultural missions are taking a more holistic approach to ministry. Practical theology has laid a foundation for women to use their gifts and talents both in the church and beyond. The mission goes beyond the four walls of a congregation, beyond a small circle of church women. If we all, male and female, are created in God's image, we are intended to participate in God's way of being. We are participants with God in the re-creation of humanity in reconciliation, solidarity, and community.[13]

---

13. Garcia, "Women's Ministries," 32.

Ted Engstrom writes, "Women need the encouragement and acceptance of men and other women to become all that God would have them to be. Many of them would surprise themselves, as well as their colleagues, at how well they might carry out an executive position."[14] Today in Global Missions, this has become a reality. Women can and do serve in every area of Church of God missions with full authority and acceptance. While there are some areas of the world where women still do not have as much freedom as men to minister, women today enjoy unprecedented opportunities to obey God's call in cross-cultural ministry.

Without women's skills of servant leadership and their sensitivity to the call of God, without their financial support of mission causes and their disciplined study of the world and its needs, the cross-cultural mission efforts of the church would greatly suffer. Let us continue to recognize and celebrate the vital contributions women make to cross-cultural mission and ensure they are accepted, trained, and empowered to take the gospel to every people, to every place, and to every generation.

About the Authors

Dondeena Caldwell lived for four years in Syria and Egypt while her parents, William and Vada Fleenor, were missionaries there. She received her bachelor's degree from Anderson University and her master's degree from the University of the Americas in Mexico City, Mexico.

The first pastorate for Dondeena and Maurice Caldwell was a Hispanic congregation, Belvedere Church of God in Los Angeles, California. She assisted in the founding of the Bible institute in Saltillo, Mexico, La Buena Tierra; and the Bible institute in Curitiba, Brazil, La Boa Terra. Dondeena has served as a career missionary most of her life. She served in Mexico for eleven years and in Brazil for eight years. She has been a linguist, teacher, translator, and editor.

---

14. Engstrom and Dayton, "Best Man for the Job," 15.

She trained Brazilian leaders in Christian education and music. She was involved in the publications *La Trompeta* (Spanish) and *A Trombeta* (Portuguese). She edited the National Women's Society bulletin, *0 Desafio*. She also participated in the translation and publication of Spanish and Portuguese hymn books.

Kathi Sellers is an ordained minister who served in pastoral ministry for eighteen years and as a missionary serving in Costa Rica for sixteen years. She now serves Global Missions in the area of missionary recruitment and member care. Kathi is married to Wayne Sellers, and they have two adult daughters.

CHAPTER 8

Contemporary Women and Their Calls to Ministry

Abby Smith

I am the epitome of someone who came into ministry kicking and screaming. I grew up in a ministry home—the daughter, granddaughter, and great-granddaughter of Church of God pastors—and while I never resented that upbringing, I also never thought of vocational ministry as something I wanted to do. When I started college, I had a plan for what I wanted to do with my life, and I was determined not to steer off course. During the first year and a half, however, God began to stir in my heart and show me that my plans were not the best. Instead of going to law school, as I had originally planned, I felt called to go to seminary after graduation to pursue some form of work in ministry. I wrestled with this call, but once I was able to set aside my pride and my fears, the Lord used confirmation after confirmation to show me that I had made the right decision.

Over the years that followed, God began to reveal another piece of what this ministry would look like: a call to overseas missions.

Again I resisted, but God slowly began to soften my heart and open my mind to the possibility of working in Latin America. While I was in seminary, I did a summer internship in Bogotá, Colombia, and fell in love with the people there. I felt my heart stirred with the knowledge that more needed to be done, and I felt God calling me to go. Once I accepted that call, the months that followed were nothing short of miraculous, as God opened door after door to help me get to Colombia as quickly as possible after graduation. During those months, I also began the credentialing process with Indiana Ministries, recognizing that a significant part of my calling included a pastoral component. I also wrestled with that part of the call at times, wondering how it would fit into the ministry context in Colombia, but I have come to understand that the call to the pastorate is so much more than a call to preach or to be the figurehead leader of a congregation. It is not a badge of honor but a servant's towel, and we who understand ourselves as pastors must learn that we are first and foremost called to model Christ's humble servanthood and to teach those placed in our sphere of influence to do the same.

Working in Colombia has been a tremendous challenge and a tremendous blessing. Some of the ministry has been very different than what I expected, but I am privileged to work with families, to encourage and equip pastors, and to teach believers in the Church of God and other denominations about the importance of living out God's mission of reconciliation in their daily lives and contexts. I continue to learn and grow in my understanding of what God has called me to do and have come to realize that the process will continue for the rest of my life. God, with great wisdom, has shown me only one piece at a time, helping me learn to walk in faith and trust as I strive to be the Christ-follower and minister I have been called to be. Although I do not know what the future has in store, I have seen God's hand of faithfulness constantly at work, and I will continue to put my trust in the One who walks before, behind, and beside me every step of the way.

Carron Odokara

"I in them and you in me. May they be brought to complete unity to let the world know that you sent me and have loved them even as you have loved me" (John 17:23 NIV1984). My calling is to live out this prayer of Jesus. Everything I am and all God has allowed me to experience have birthed in me a desire to see the church be one so the world sees the One in us, Jesus.

I am the daughter of a man from Nigeria and a Caucasian woman from rural Ithaca, Michigan. My parents were an unlikely pair who were discouraged from marriage by their families, friends, and pastors. They married during a time when the country and the church talked about the theory of unity but practiced something far less. If my parents had listened to those around them, I would not be here—but I am.

I grew up in a world of many cultures in the communities, schools, and work environments I experienced, but not in the church. My father had a distaste for the church after a negative experience in an African American congregation shortly after he came to this country. My mother, who was returning to the faith her parents had taught her, took me to a Caucasian church because that was the type of church my father would allow us to attend. For many years, I attended churches whose primary cultural diversity came from my walking through the door. A few times, supposedly well-meaning church people suggested that my mother should consider going elsewhere. But we did find churches that were caring and welcoming and that were interested in utilizing my mother's musical talents on the organ.

After my father left us and the country during my high school years, my grandmother, my mother, and I became my only immediate family. My grandmother and my mother taught me about Jesus through their words and through their lives. I did not appreciate until later all they taught me as a child and how much support and encouragement they gave to my faith. In college, I had to establish my own identity and figure out what I believed. I searched and questioned, and the process ended up reinforcing my faith in Jesus Christ—thanks, in part, to the faithful women who raised me.

Even with faith in Jesus, I had questions about the Church of God, but there were some intriguing distinctives. I was excited by the diversity in the Church of God with African American congregations and Caucasian congregations, since I relate to both. Unfortunately, I was forced to choose one cultural group at a time because of the persistent lines of separation. There were also gender distinctives I found interesting. If work and school did not limit my potential value because I am female, why should the church? God can gift and use females or males in any capacity he chooses. The teachings of the Church of God do not limit the possibilities for my service and ministry. Unfortunately, some people do not practice what we teach. The unity of believers for ministry and the opportunity to reach across cultural and gender divides appealed to me and made me thankful to be a third generation in the Church of God.

As I entered my last year as an undergraduate, God was working on me. I point back to one night at camp meeting in St. Louis, Michigan, when I went to the altar. There, God gave me a desire for his ministry. I did not know what ministry meant or how it would look. It was a scary concept that I did not share with people for many years. In response to God's prompting, I explored aspects of ministry as he provided opportunities, yet I ran from it at the same time. Ministry doors opened to allow me serve for a month doing an inner-city mission in Kingston, Jamaica, and to be an interim after the youth pastor at my mother's church left. However, after my grandmother died, my focus shifted to what I perceived as a more logical path. I finished my undergraduate and graduate degrees in engineering, and then began a job in information technology. I thought I would serve God on the side as I could find the time.

Years later, my mother died and God got my attention once again. My focus and priorities changed to the next steps for ministry, so I attended seminary at a school near my job. After a few semesters, it became evident that the seminary did not support women in ministry, even though they were glad to take my money and have me in their classes. God used that time to teach me and to teach them. Sometimes I held my tongue, but other times I tried to gently express an alternate perspective about women in ministry. My breaking point came in my senior theology seminar when I no longer cared whether they expelled me from school over my views. Following an assignment to debate a classmate about the role of women, I was questioned by fellow students who had never been exposed to the possibility of women ministers. Then I was challenged to debate my own professor, who interrogated me about my God-given spiritual gifts, about the ministry positions God used me to fill, and about my biblical exegesis. It was only a battle in the war, but fortunately my master of divinity degree was not one of the casualties. I graduated with *summa cum laude* honors and with the expository communication award (since women are not allowed to be called preachers). God placed me there to experience the challenges faced by a woman in ministry, and he used me to show other students that God can use women in any capacity he chooses.

My service to date has not been as an ordained minister. (At the time of this writing, I am working on the ordination process.) However, God has opened doors to use me as a layperson. In my local church, I started by teaching and preaching, and grew into leadership as chair of the church council. In state ministry, God allowed me to serve on committees to address social concerns, to coordinate leadership development training, and to chair the state's general assembly. In national involvement, I was given the opportunity to serve on the Ministries Council and currently serve as the vice chair. Locally, I am an associate pastor serving part time at a multicultural church while waiting to see what God has for me next.

God has given me so many opportunities to be involved in his work. All along the way, people have questioned whether I should be doing what I was doing. Sometimes I would question as well! However, as I reflect back, I know God has opened doors to do things I never would have dreamed possible. God will continue to work through me or in spite of me. God has been with me through many challenges in life and in the church setting, and he has strengthened my desire for unity in the church. I continue to pray, as Jesus did, for God's church to be one, united in reaching out and changing the world for him.

Shannon New Spangler

You know those people who have known since they were born that they were going to be in ministry? I am not one of those people. In fact, I grew up in a pastor's home and so never had *any* intention of being in ministry. I knew how much work it was and more importantly, I saw how it disrupted normal living.

At eighteen, I went to Anderson University as a mathematics major with the goal of being a teacher. I was good at math but didn't love it—there was no passion there. But I loved being at AU. I got involved in a lot of areas and enjoyed life on campus.

As every freshman at AU must, I took an "Intro to the Bible" course. I heard things in that course that I had never heard in Sunday school, stories that intrigued me and passages that brought me to tears. The Bible drew me in: I loved it, I loved the stories, I loved the poetry, I loved the lessons. In my second semester, something began to move inside of me (I understand it now as holy discontent), and before my sophomore year I changed my major to Bible and religion. Even then, I had no idea what God had in store for me. I was certain I had no business being in ministry, but I was just as certain that the Bible was my passion and that my life must have that passion in it. I took the classes I had to take but truly thrived in biblical studies.

Throughout my last two years at college, I heard a lot about "the call." I struggled with where God was calling me. I talked to family, friends, and mentors. I thought I could be a pastor's wife or maybe a missionary. I was still uncertain what place God had for me in ministry.

Upon graduating from college, I went into a youth pastorate. I truly loved the kids and loved the ministry but still felt something was not quite in sync. I decided to go back to school for more education, to try to discover where God wanted me to be. I commuted for a year, three hours one way every week. It was during this time that I heard God leading me in the direction of being a senior pastor.

After only a year a half, I left the youth pastorate to attend Anderson University School of Theology full time for my master of divinity degree. I went to school part time and worked as a waitress to make it through. As hard as it was, however, I gained more and more assurance in my call. I developed my gifts, soaked in the education, and began preparing for a life in the ministry.

During my time in seminary, a wise mentor told me, "If you can do anything else, do it. Ministry is hard." I searched myself over those years and became confident to my core that I could not legitimately do anything else. I was certain God had given me a ministry and had a plan for me in the work of the church.

However, being confident in my call did not guarantee me a ministry position. In my last year of seminary I began the search for a church to serve. I sent letters, I emailed, I called, I made contacts and spoke to people who could help me. I spent increasing hours on websites searching for information. I graduated in May from seminary with no prospects and began substitute teaching. I got dozens upon dozens of rejections from churches all over the country. A few places called for more information and I had several interviews, but nothing panned out. I began to doubt myself and I got angry with God.

Six months after graduation, I received a call from a pastor friend who asked me to consider being his youth pastor. I was in a place of desperation and depression and wondered whether I should accept the offer. Fortunately, after discussion with my husband, we determined that I could not reject God's call on my life for something easy. And so I waited. I prayed. I cried. I kept searching.

A few months later, I got a call from a church that had gotten my name from their state office. We met with them several times over the next few months, and in April we came to candidate at Harvest Point Church in Lordstown, Ohio. They voted to invite us to serve here, and we came the first of June, more than a year after my graduation.

I have been at Harvest Point for more than three years, and we feel wonderfully blessed. I am certain that the waiting resulted in a perfect placement for me and for this church, for this season in both of our lives.

Adrienne Holmes

The late James Brown co-wrote a song called "It's a Man's Man's Man's World." When God called me to preach, that was exactly what I discovered: preaching is a man's world.

In 1976, God dropped into my spirit Isaiah 61:1: "The Spirit of the Lord God is upon Me, because the Lord has anointed Me to preach good tidings to the poor" (NKJV). I tried to ignore it, but it kept ringing over and over in my spirit. So I prayed. About a week later I went to my pastor, the late Dr. R. L. Fuller, a Southern Baptist preacher, and told him God was calling me to preach. He told me to go back and pray again. I did as he instructed. I went back. I prayed. And Isaiah 61:1 kept ringing in my spirit. I went back to Dr. Fuller two more times, and two more times he instructed me, "Go back and pray." After the fourth time of going back and praying, I told Dr. Fuller I was called to *teach*. He agreed, because "God doesn't call women to preach." I thought to myself, "Well, God is surely calling me."

I began teaching in adult Sunday school, but instead of teaching I always ended up preaching. So they moved me to the pre-K Sunday school class. But guess what? It didn't matter, because there, too, I preached. From the pre-K class they moved me to the substitute teacher's class so they could control when I taught and so I could be under the scrutiny of the deacons, but the Holy Spirit didn't care who was watching or who was listening—when the Spirit set upon me, I preached. Whenever I opened my mouth in church, I preached.

It was not until the Lord moved me to Indianapolis, Indiana, in 1988 that I was able to openly exercise my gift to preach, but even now I am occasionally faced with the thought, *Preaching and pastoring is a man's world.*

When God really began to deal with me regarding preaching, I was playing the organ in South Calvary Baptist Church, working as minister of music. I told the pastor there that God had called me to preach, but again I was faced with the same old adage, "God doesn't call women to preach." Well, one Sunday for this pastor's anniversary he had a visiting pastor come to preach. My pastor had evidently told this man what I had said about being called to preach, because from the pulpit he quoted the Baptist preacher's favorite Scripture to block women from preaching, 1 Timothy 3:1–2: "If a man desires the position of a bishop, he desires a good work. A bishop then must be blameless, the husband of one wife..." (NKJV). This preacher man said, "If a woman can get past this scripture and be the husband of one wife, then she can preach and I will sit down."

I left the church with my five small adopted children, got in my van, and thought I was headed home—but when I came to myself, I was almost in Chicago. As I drove, I began to pray, asking God how could I get past that scripture. I knew God was calling me to preach, but only a man could be the husband of one wife. I needed the Spirit to give me a defense of this scripture. As I drove, God began to speak into my spirit. God said, "What was Solomon's demise?" and I said, "All of his wives and his concubines." Then God said, "Solomon had more than one wife, as did many others in Scripture. A woman cannot be the wife of more than one husband, but a man can be the husband of more than one wife. When a man has more than one wife, he does not have proper time for the things of the Lord because his attention is divided. However, this does not apply to a woman—especially a single woman" (which I am). From that point on, I accepted my calling and have been preaching ever since—in a man's world.

Prayer has always been at the center of everything I do. My mother was a praying woman, and I too am a praying woman. With every venture God has called me into, I've gone into prayer first, asking for confirmation of the Lord's leading, and then I've stepped out in faith. For instance, I always wanted to go to college. But when I graduated from high school with a four-year scholarship to Fisk University, my mother said, "Black people don't go to college, they go to work." So off to work I went. But in 1999, God blessed me to graduate from Crossroads Bible College as the only woman with a pastoral studies degree. I knew I was on the right track.

When I knew God was calling me to pastor, I prayed to be sent someplace I could learn so I wouldn't embarrass God or myself. And the Lord sent me to Victory Memorial United Methodist Church to sit under the tutelage of Pastor James Mulholland. Pastor Mulholland taught me virtually everything I know about ministry. From there God sent me to my first full-time pastorate at Bell's Chapel Church of God, where I have served for more than twelve years. I also planted and pastor Abounding Grace Church of God.

Pastoring hasn't been easy for me. I have been shut out of many circles, but when God calls you, God becomes your circle. I don't look for the accolades of man, for the approval of man, but I am working, doing what God has called me to do, to please God so that one day I can hear God say to me, "Adrienne, my servant, well done."

Jael JieMin Tang

"Simon answered, 'Master, we've worked hard all night and haven't caught anything. But because you say so, I will let down the nets'" (Luke 5:5 NIV). Airports rank pretty high on my favorite places in the world. Folks coming and going. Welcome. See you again. Chapters closing. New beginnings.

But airports have not always been my favorite place. The airport in Los Angeles, for instance. I was reluctantly moving halfway across the world for the first time for college, and an eight-hour layover listening to the public service announcement about unattended baggage did nothing for my need for familiarity.

That was eight years ago now. What I did not know at the time was that those eight hours were the beginning of an adventure. Only a few days before, my pastor in Singapore had commissioned me with the words from Luke 5, where Jesus called his first disciples. "Jesus told the men to put out into deep water. You do the same, Jael. Go a little further."

Growing up, I had assumed life was going to be predictable. I would finish studies in Singapore and someday become a music teacher. I acknowledged a Greater Being in control of my life that the adults called "God." They were impressed that I looked like I was pursuing God, since I played the piano in church as good church-going kids do and was a good student who knew the difference between Abraham, David, and Paul. The Bible answers came easy, but I had become convinced that authentically following this God demanded more than just being a good kid. But what did that mean? I felt like I was faking faith, and I was frustrated.

Then predictability got pulled from under my feet. I flunked out of school and my good-kid record was no longer clean. My senior pastor then told me about Anderson University, where his sons had gone to school. "They have a good music program there; it might just be what you're looking for."

In the airport in LA for eight hours, I still assumed I would eventually graduate from Anderson and go back to my predictable life in Singapore. Little did I realize that *predictable* was about to disappear from my vocabulary.

Several university-sponsored missions trips later, it was becoming clear to me that I loved cross-cultural service. Coupled with discouraging experiences in the local church, I reached a point where I no longer wanted anything to do with predictable church life. I knew I needed to go to seminary, but I was burnt out from academics and church, and I needed a break. Because I was not a U.S. citizen, my options for short-term missions were practically nonexistent. I knew then that my path would look very different from my American contemporaries.

I ended up taking an administrative assistant job at Global Missions, the missionary-sending arm of the Church of God in North America, while also serving as worship assistant in a small local church (what all good church-going kids with a church music degree do). I continued trying to bargain my way out of going to seminary even as folks I met as part of the job tried to convince me it was a great idea.

I started the school year kicking and screaming. Nonetheless, my passion for cross-cultural ministry took on a whole new slant as I watched cross-cultural ministers and their families return exhausted from the mission field. What kept me in the program was the realization that I would be better equipped to serve them if I had a seminary degree.

Again, I made the mistake of assuming that life would be predictable after seminary. At the end of my second year, I had the opportunity to spend three months in Berlin as part of a team exploring what it means to live as a Christ-centered community in a postmodern, post-Christian culture. The only thing I knew about that three months was that I would be having coffee with women who worked the streets. I did not even know why I was going, aside from the fact that the doors kept opening. I was confident I would come back, finish seminary, and keep trying to create space for exhausted cross-cultural workers to take a break.

As I boarded the plane for Germany, the words from my pastor in Singapore echoed again in my mind. "Go a little further, Jael." During those three months in Berlin, I came to understand that ministry is never about one fixed place or task. For me, the radical thing about the Berlin experience was realizing the concept of a Christ-centered community can be transplanted to just about anywhere in the world. The frameworks of these communities will look different, but life change happens where folks are given space for their personhood to be embraced regardless of the walk of life they come from.

While finishing seminary the following year, I found myself exploring the possibility of accepting a children's ministry position in Auckland, New Zealand. To begin, I was still reluctant to work in a church. But even more, I had always understood the church as an intergenerational entity, so to narrow my focus to a specific age-group—and one that I had no prior experience with—made me even more hesitant. Yet the words came back again: "Go a little further, Jael."

I realized then that the conviction I'd had as a kid about the demands of authentically following God is fairly orthodox. Following God means going a little further as the seasons change. It requires the response Simon gave: "Because you say so, I will let down the nets."

Airports never annoy me these days. In fact, even the public service announcements are a welcome reminder of a faithful God who will walk with me as I go a little further.

CHAPTER 9

Women, Change, and the Church

BY JUANITA EVANS LEONARD AND MARYANN HAWKINS

I n earlier chapters, we have examined specific biblical, theological, and historical data regarding the empowerment and leadership of women in the Church of God. These life stories, biblical evidence, and ethical concerns have been lifted up to point the way for further discussion and exploration.

In this chapter, we will explore leadership issues facing the Church of God as we move beyond the first decade of the twenty-first century. Many of the ideas discussed here were also considered in the early 1970s and mid-1980s. In many ways, the conversation remains relevant only because we seem to be stuck; by failing to respond decades ago, we kicked the problem down the road and now find ourselves revisiting the same questions and possible solutions. We will look here at the role of women and suggest strategies to intentionally change the status quo. We offer these diagnoses and strategies as seeds for change that must be cultivated through prayer, discussion, and action by women and men who are called and gifted to lead the church into the future.

Relationships

The closing lines of the familiar marriage service end with these words: "to preserve an inviolable fidelity, and to see to it, that what God has joined thus together, man never puts asunder."[1] Paul, writing to the Christians in Rome, said:

> With eyes wide open to the mercies of God, I beg you, my brothers, as an act of intelligent worship, to give him your bodies, as a living sacrifice, consecrated to him and acceptable by him. Don't let the world around you squeeze you into its own mold, but let God remold your minds from within so that the plan of God for you is good, meets all his demands and moves toward the goal of true maturity. (Rom 12:1–2 JBP)

The lesson in both these admonitions warns against that which could cause either a man or woman not to fulfill the purpose of God in his or her life. Whether we are considering the "inviolable fidelity" required to sustain a lifelong marriage or keeping our "eyes wide open to the mercies of God" as we follow Christ, the call of God must be diligently and persistently obeyed or we risk trading God's high call for a mess of pottage (Gen 25:29–34). The church stands in grave danger should we persist in disallowing, either consciously or unconsciously, the giftedness and "called-ness" of women for partnership in the church's life, leadership structure, and mission. The lack of women's full presence in all dimensions of the church's life has manifested again and again in faith communities who were, at their beginnings, open to women exercising all the spiritual gifts: apostles, teachers, administrators, helps, mercy, and so on. As these groups, including the Church of God, became organized and institutionalized, their structures began to look more and more like the social institutions of the culture; the

---

1. Hilcox, *Star Book for Ministers*, 215.

church adopted society's structural norms. "Our recorded heritage reveals that there have always been women preachers in the Church of God. They are accepted without debate. We have had decades when our culture influenced our movement to discourage women in pastoral ministry."[2] Kari Torgensen Malcolm writes about the mid-nineteenth century Holiness revivals:

Because of the emphasis on declaring what God has done, silence became almost a sin, as Phoebe Upham suggests: "To impart what one receives from God is the outgoing life of the new Christ nature…How opposed then to the new Christ nature, and to God's word, is the sealing of woman's lips in the public exercises of the Church."[3]

D. S. Warner, like John Wesley, Charles G. Finney, and Phoebe Palmer, emphasized the sanctification of the Holy Spirit on the believer's life. Pentecost was central to the experience of holiness. Believers expected to be empowered with gifts that would enable them to witness with "holy boldness" to the end that the good news would convince men and women of sin, leading to repentance and reconciliation. Church historian John W. V. Smith wrote:

There was never a time in the history of the movement in fact, when women were not considered an essential part of the leadership. It was a striking aspect of the early days to see women functioning on the same level as men. Forty years before the time of woman's suffrage on a national level a great company of women were preaching, singing, writing and helping to determine the policies in this religious reformation movement.[4]

In 1902, *Familiar Names and Faces* was published. Of the two hundred first-generation leaders of the Church of God reformation movement, fifty (25 percent) were women. By the time the suffrage

---

2. McCutcheon, "Lady in the Pulpit," 5–6.

3. Malcolm, *Women at the Crossroads*, 127.

4. John V. W. Smith, *Heralds of a Brighter Day*, 125.

movement gained momentum in the 1920s, women made up 32 percent of those acknowledged as pastoral leaders in the Church of God. In the next two decades, however, the charismatic (dynamic) nature of leadership changed. Agency structures emerged and the professionalization process for clergy was adopted. The advances made by women were already being lost. The chart below, based on Sharon Sawyer's 1976 research, shows the sharp decline from 1925 to 1945:[5]

Year	Number of Congregations	Number of Women Pastors	Percentage of Congregations
1905	353	50	14%
1925	685	220	32%
1945	1,572	112	7%
1965	2,276	100	4%
1975	2,905	100	3%
2013	2,145	238	11%

The fifty years between 1925 and 1975 were bleak indeed for women called to pastoral leadership. As the reform movement developed institutional structures, doors once wide open to women closed almost completely. The dominant cultural notions about women's and men's appropriate roles persisted and were exacerbated following World War II. Although women had successfully stepped into work and ministry shoes that men had filled before the conflict, at the war's end, women were pressured to abandon these roles and return to the home. Malcolm suggests this pressure reflected the "longing of society to go back to the 'good ole days.'"[6]

Diagnosis: From Pain to Problems to Change

In the wake of World War II, the press of the world's mold began to overtake the movement—and not just where women were concerned. It is not possible to talk honestly about this era of Church

---

5. Sawyer, "Women Pastors in the Church of God," 2.

6. Malcolm, *Women at the Crossroads*, 137.

of God history without talking about both sexism and racism. Black men and women, as well as white women, were marginalized by the wider society and within the church. Addressing the sociological development of the Church of God in *Where the Saints Have Trod*, Clear writes:

In its early years the sect often grows phenomenally, because it offers dramatic answers to questions which deeply bother potential adherents. But in the process of answering the questions it tends to produce conditions which diminish its sectarian form. Created to fill a pressing need, the sect meets the need successfully, and in doing so it makes itself obsolete. In most cases, of course, the negativistic sect-form gives way to accommodation patterns, so that the organization continues to serve the same group of people, developing new institutional forms as the needs of the people change. Starting as a conflict group, it ultimately becomes an accommodating group.[7]

Echoing Clear, anthropologist-missiologist Paul Hiebert observes, "Institutions, like people, go through cycles of growth, maturation, and 'hardening of the categories.' The result often is a loss of vitality and life they once had."[8] He goes on to describe the process of institutionalization in this way:

First, the founding parents of an institution often pay a high price to join it, and take personal risk. They join together in a bond or fellowship of high intensity, and tremendous purpose and fellowship. The second generation is raised inside the organization and this makes them radically different. To stay in is the easiest course with little sacrifice. Nevertheless they experience vicariously the commitment and vision of their parents and often have a high commitment to the institution. The third generation is more removed from the founders and has less

---

7. Clear, *Where the Saints Have Trod*, 3.
8. Hiebert, "Phenomenology and Institutions," 112.

of their vision. Nominalism enters, and many stay in because it is the course of least resistance. The result is a growing loss of interest, a shift in goals and institutionalization. The fourth generation and on are well entrenched and the institution for them is a way of life. They have much invested in it in terms of their own identity and want to maintain it not for what it does in ministry for the world, but what it does for them as persons.[9]

Women received the franchise to vote in 1920 and there was every hope that participation in the political arena also meant society was ready for women to participate in all spheres of activity. Yet history shows that change did not come quickly and, sadly, the church reflected society. The *Gospel Trumpet*, a Church of God periodical, recorded activities of women on the overseas mission field, but it referenced few ministry activities of women in the United States. Women evangelists became fewer in number as the century progressed. There were exceptions, such as Mother Emma Meyer (1894–1920), of Louisville, Kentucky; Birdie Smith (1932–46), of Akron, Ohio; Minna Jarrett (1937–57), of Vancouver, Washington; and Lillie McCutcheon (1947–89), of Newton Falls, Ohio. These women were, against the odds, longtime pastors of established congregations.

By the early 1960s, the feminist movement and the sexual revolution began to gain steam. The civil rights movement was in full swing, and the nation was embroiled in a controversial war in Southeast Asia. There was ferment in the land, and women reared in the Church of God who had heard the call of God found the church unresponsive to their gifts. And so women took the work of love and reconciliation of Jesus into other settings; union halls, social work agencies, hospitals, and educational institutions both at home and overseas—these became their pulpits and places of service. While United States cities burned, women began to ask difficult questions of the church. Lay women and those few ordained by the institution had responded to God's call in the very churches

---

9. Ibid., 113.

that now had no place for them. And so they began once more to "cry out" as Nora Hunter had in an earlier generation.

What had transpired in the Church of God was documented in other communions of faith within the Holiness traditions. Nancy Hardesty writes:

> Holiness and Pentecostal groups, however, became preoc-cupied with institution building: churches, denominational structures, publishing houses, colleges, even seminaries. In the beginning they despised seminary-educated ministers; now they coveted one for their own congregation. Begun often as churches of the urban poor, they [women] were again squeezed out of leadership by the values of the dominant culture. They were evangelists and missionaries, home and foreign, but they were not pastors of larger churches, denominational execu-tives, or seminary professors.[10]

Vision had given way to routine. Organizational maintenance was substituted for evangelization and the healing of the ills of people and society. More effort was spent on maintaining the orga-nization and less on ministry to the world. Flexibility gave way to inflexibility. Those in power whose identities were entwined with position and status had a vested interest in maintaining the status quo of the institution.

By the 1970s and 1980s, a passion for people had given way to a focus on programs. Success was measured in programs and buildings. As the institutional machinery continued to grow, white women and ethnic minorities were increasingly detached and alienated from the church. The core composition of the "flying ministries" of early days of the Church of God was gone. Imper-sonalization was rampant, and the majority clergy controlled the institution; the church was no longer sensitive to women's needs and goals for service. The egalitarian informality of the church's be-ginnings had hardened into an entrenched hierarchy. The sense of

---

10. Hardesty, *Women Called to Witness*, 159.

camaraderie as "the whole people of God" had all but died. There remained an intellectual assent to women in ministry, but the realized vision needed once more to be fanned into flame by the Holy Spirit's power and those empowered by the Word.

The ray of hope for women through the twentieth century was the emergence of the lay Women's Missionary Society, which became the Women of the Church of God in 1974. The constituency of Women of the Church of God was a vast, largely untapped, potential leadership resource for the life of the church. Some of the group's strength lay in the fact that it was outside the hierarchical family of church agencies. Led during the late 1960s and 1970s by an ordained minister, Nellie J. Snowden, and a talented, energetic staff (Marie Meyer, Joyce Nisely, Johanna Bridges, Nell McManus, and Kay Shively), this grassroots network of women helped shape the conversation about women in ministry by asking questions: What are women doing with God's call on their lives? Are women a part (or not) of the decision-making bodies of the church? Are women being (or not) invited by congregations to be pastors? Are women entering Church of God colleges and seminaries to prepare for ministry?

Those in power had become more interested in what they could get out of the institution than in what they could contribute to it. But women of the movement slowly, haltingly at times, began to ask their questions more boldly. By the Spirit's power, the renewal process of the church began and women began to rediscover their voices.

The past three decades have seen increased cooperation between the Executive Council, the Women of the Church of God, Anderson University School of Theology, and other groups to address the disconnect between the theology and tradition of the Church of God and its lived reality with regard to women in ministry and leadership. Various initiatives have opened more doors for women to education and ordination, but as late as 2009, Dr. Ronald Duncan, general director of Church of God Ministries until 2013, expressed dismay at a report showing that almost 70 percent of clergywomen who were licensed or ordained were without a place of service. They were listed in the *Yearbook* as "ministers"—not pastors, not associates, not evangelists or educators—simply ministers. In a research project concerning leadership development of clergywomen (2000–2003), survey respondents reported, again and again, that their résumés were not considered for pastoral ministry because they were women.[11] Alarmingly, it appears that many district or state structures do not even question a church that will not consider a female as pastor. In June 2010, area administrators received lists of both the names of women "ministers" and churches without pastors in their particular areas. Only two area administrators spoke to the presenter about changing their processes for consulting with churches without pastors to ensure that called and qualified women are considered by search committees for pastoral placement. Even more alarming, several local Church of God congregations have, since 2005, moved to change their by-laws to forbid women from serving on pastoral staff or as congregational elders. Are we moving forward or backward when it comes to women in ministry?

A Plan for Change

The Church of God needs the Holy Spirit to renew our minds with respect to the gifts of women called of God for pastoral leadership. In order to see this vision through to completion, it will take a radical, countercultural decision to act on biblical imperatives.

When the walls of partition fall—the obstacles that block the creative use of women's spiritual gifts for the good of God's kingdom—it will be because the majority of those who influence the church have abandoned "ideas which are in accord with their interest, needs, or existing attitudes."[12] It may be that some of these leaders and influencers will, with the Spirit's help, renew their minds and reorient their priorities, even if it means abandoning the comfortable status quo. But others may need your help! Will you be an

---

11. Hawkins, *Clergywomen of the Church of God.*
12. Rogers and Shoemaker, *Communication of Innovations,* 105.

agent of change and renewal in the Church of God? Consider the following ideas for taking action:

- Identify the kinds of barriers that block women in ministry and the kind of filters that are used to maintain the system in the congregation, state assembly, or in the national agencies and offices.
- Select and engage in dialogue with key members of your community (network) about the giftedness of women in pastoral leadership of the church.
- Discuss the issue of women in leadership with those in your immediate network of friends—consider the need for pastoral leadership in the Church of God, discuss the biblical and historical foundation for the role of women in leadership.
- Call together the women and men within your church, state, or region who are working with these concerns, and note the issues and the opportunities.

As a change agent, it is important to remember the three types of people who will help you to change the status quo to include the idea of women in ministry.[13]

The *Innovators* are risk-takers. They tend to be intelligent, are travelers, read a lot, use outside sources of information, and often are receptive to the influence of outside change agents. Innovators are daring and experimental and have the ability to understand and apply complex concepts. They are comfortable and able to cope with a high degree of uncertainty. Talk to innovators in terms of the church's future, emphasizing how women will help lead the church through the exciting and uncertain times ahead.

The *Resisters* in most social systems (which includes the church) have some members who take an active role as critics of innovation or change, but most often these persons are defenders of the system as it is. Usually they are self-appointed guardians of moral, ethical,

---

13. Havelock, *Change Agents Guide*, 120.

and legal standards. As preservers of the social order, resisters play a useful part. They resist alien influences in our society; the analogy of antibodies in the bloodstream comes to mind. Talk to resisters in terms of the church's past, highlighting the strong tradition of women in ministry that is essential to our identity.

The *Leaders* are held in high esteem within the church nationally, regionally, and locally and are key to unlocking women in ministry. Opinion leaders listen to the innovators and resisters, and attempt to get a balanced understanding of the issue. They wish to be champions of the innovations whose time has come.

Who are these opinion leaders? They are pastors, state and local presidents of Christian Women Connection, chairpersons of committees within the local congregation or the state, regional, and national church. Regional pastors and executives of national agencies are central to leadership decisions and to the prevailing status quo. Prayerfully consider all the relationships in your church network to identify the opinion leaders who can help you catalyze change. Depending on their position and gifting, some of these leaders will be "legitimators," those who help people accept and feel positive about women in active ministry roles. Others will serve as "facilitators" who make necessary policy and system changes to make room for a new paradigm. Still others, the "gatekeepers," will extend opportunities and open doors that were previously inaccessible to women.

The Spirit is guiding the vision for women to preach and teach, to lead and serve. God's people can no longer disobey the revealed Word by operating in the church with the world's values. We must no longer restrict the spiritual gifts of any believer because of gender, race, economic status, physical handicap, or age. God originates gifts and calling, without respect to our worldly divisions. It is high time we who claim the tradition of holiness are led by the Holy Spirit rather than anyone or anything else.

Where the Spirit of the Lord is, there is peace, power, perseverance, and praise. God is raising up a great company of women in this generation to take the message of holiness, unity, and love into all the world. You too are called to stand and share, whether you are female or male, young or mature, rich or poor. Answer God's call, and lend your hand and voice to women who seek to do likewise.

About the Authors

Juanita Leonard is an ordained minister of the Church of God and professor emeritus of the Anderson University School of Theology. She has a master's degree in social service from Indiana University, a postgraduate certificate in marriage and family counseling from the University of Minnesota, and a PhD in intercultural studies from Fuller Theological Seminary. In 1986, she received the Distinguished Service Award from the American Association of Marriage and Family Therapists.

MaryAnn Hawkins is an ordained minister of the Church of God and professor of intercultural studies at Anderson University School of Theology. She is also the convener for Qara: Church of God Women in Ministry, an organization for mobilizing and networking women clergy in the church. MaryAnn serves as the Church of God representative to the Board of Directors for the Wesleyan-Holiness Women Clergy and is a member of the Wesleyan-Holiness Consortium Steering Committee. Hawkins completed her master's degree in leadership at Azusa Pacific University and her PhD in intercultural studies at Fuller Theological Seminary. MaryAnn is a sought-after speaker and teacher on leadership, mission, postmodern ministry, and women in ministry.

Women and Men—
Partners in Ministry

GENESIS 1:27-28; GALATIANS 3:26-28;
1 TIMOTHY 2:11-15

*Transcript of a sermon by David Sebastian,
dean of Anderson University School of Theology*

God will never bless this church as long as there are women in leadership." When those words echoed through the sanctuary during an annual business meeting, you could have heard a pin drop.

From where I stood, I could see the facial expressions of the congregation. Some heads snapped in the direction of the one making the comment as if to say, "Who would make such an archaic remark? Other people stared straight ahead. They knew why women were in leadership, but they held their breath hoping there would not be division in the church. Still other folks glanced at me with raised eyebrows, "Why *were* we electing women to serve as congregational leaders?"

My response was short probably because I was shocked by the unsolicited statement. "Our church tradition has always recognized gifted women. This is not an item for discussion at the annual business meeting, but I would be happy to talk with you about your concern at a later time." I swallowed hard. Ballots were marked. The business meeting concluded.

The next week my outspoken parishioner made an appointment to see me. His yellow pad was filled with notes. He said, "Pastor, I really like you and the church, but…!" Have you ever had anyone say, "I like you, but…? What follows usually mutes the "I like you" part of the statement. He said, "I think our church is wrong about women in ministry. If we continue in disobedience, I fear we will lose the blessing of God and our church will die."

"Pastor," he went on to say, "*everybody* knows women are inferior to men when it comes to leadership." His matter-of-fact approach reminded me of the position of the church in the Middle Ages when it was said that women lacked "eminence."[1] For example, Thomas Aquinas advanced this eminence idea based partly upon the science of Aristotle. Aristotle suggested that male semen was white and dominant and that female menstruation was red and inferior.[2] Therefore, men were by nature superior to women. In the Middle Ages nearly everyone accepted as fact that men were by nature superior and should lead in the home, church, and government. But I thought to myself, *We are not in the Middle Ages anymore.*

I said to my guest, "I disagree. Look around you and you will see women, when given opportunity, accomplishing great things in every field of endeavor. This is not surprising to me, for in the beginning God created them in his own image, male and female he created them and told *them* to rule over the earth."[3]

"But, Pastor, you have to admit that Jesus chose only men to be his apostles." Yes, Jesus, in a patriarchal culture, chose only Jewish men.[4] However, if we use the bar of Jewish maleness, the vast majority of Christian leaders are disqualified to serve.

---

1. Wijngaards, *Ordination of Women*, 101.
2. Ibid., 103
3. Genesis 2 (NRSV).
4. Huber, *Called, Equipped, No Place to Go*, 47.

"Pastor, this is serious, you are called to guard the truth. The Bible clearly states, 'A woman is not permitted to teach or to have authority over a man.'"[5] Yes, that is what 1 Timothy 2:12 clearly states, but what it means is not so clear. For we read in the same paragraph (2:15) that "she (woman) will be saved through childbearing."

Do we really believe women are saved by having children?" What about "by grace we are saved through faith"?[6] What about women who never have children? Are they disqualified from the heavenly prize? We must be careful not to build eternal doctrines on disputed passages. What is clear is that the vast majority of verses in the Old and New Testament describe women in leadership roles while less than a handful appear to limit their service.[7]

He left my office unconvinced and eventually left the church because of our biblical position on women in leadership. But one thing he said stuck with me. "Pastor, you are called to guard the truth."

When he left my study, I opened my Bible and began to reflect once again upon 1 Timothy 2:11–15. As the letter opens the author of the Pastorals reminds Timothy "to remain in Ephesus so that you may instruct certain people not to teach any different doctrine and not to occupy themselves with myths and endless genealogies that promote speculations rather than divine training that is known by faith."[8] False teachers were in the church. Therefore, Timothy at the close of the letter is told to "guard what has been entrusted to you."[9]

While 1 Timothy does not define the content of these myths, genealogies, and speculations, there is extrabiblical evidence suggesting an early Gnostic teaching was infiltrating the church in Ephesus. For years in Ephesus the temple of Artemis had been a center for the worship of the feminine. "Cerinthius, a first-century Gnostic in Ephesus, promoted the worship of 'Authentia' as the

---

5. 1 Timothy 2:12.

6. Ephesians 2:8–9.

7. Huber, *Called, Equipped, No Place to Go*, 33.

8. 1 Timothy 1:3–5.

9. 1 Timothy 6:20.

Primal Deity from which all else derived."[10] The Pastoral letters were written to guard against these myths and speculations that were spreading from house to house like wildfire.

Instructions were given to men and women, but more lengthy instructions were given to women: "Let a woman learn in silence with full submission."[11] The shocking thing about this verse, when heard within either a Jewish or Greek context, was not "in silence with full submission" but the imperative to "let a woman learn." This ancient formula[12] "in silence and submission" did not mean a woman should not speak but rather that a learner should come peacefully under the truth that was being taught.[13] There is nothing in the verse that suggests a woman should be in submission to man but rather she is to be in submission to the truth.

The instruction continues, "I permit no woman to teach or to have authority over a man, she is to keep silent."[14] The verb "I permit no" (*epitrepo,*) is in the *present continual tense*. In other words, Paul does not say, "I will not /never permit," but rather, "I am not (now) permitting."[15] This is a huge difference. For example, there is a difference if your employer would say, "I will not/never permit employees to have a pay increase," over against saying, "I am not now permitting employees to have a pay increase."

Scholars such as Witherington and Wijngaards conclude that women were temporarily told to stop teaching until they clearly understood apostolic instruction. Wijingaards, drawing upon church tradition, affirms that for nine hundred years women taught and were involved in all aspects of Christian ministry. [16]

Richard and Catherine Kroeger drill deeper into the text and offer an alternative translation. They remind us the infinitives *to teach (didaskein)* and *to have authority (authentein)* are crucial

---

10. Kroeger and Kroeger, *I Suffer Not a Woman*, 101.

11. 1 Timothy 2:11.

12. Ibid., 32.

13. Perhaps the modern formula, "Every head bowed and every eye closed," might be a similar way to proceed reverently.

14. 1 Timothy 2:12.

15. Witherington, *Women in the Ministry of Jesus*, 226.

16. Wijngaards, *Ordination of Women*, 49.

in unlocking the meaning of this passage. For instance, wherever *to teach* (*didaskein*) is found in the Pastorals, it always has to do with content rather than mere pedagogical activity.[17] *To teach* (*didaskein*) has to do with either truth or error.

The infinitive *to have authority* (*authentein*) is only used once in the entire Bible. This begs us to question, "What was the author intending in selecting this unique word over against more commonly used words for authority or power (*kurieuein* or *exousizein*)?" Possible meanings for *authentein* outside the biblical cannon include "to be responsible for murder, to dominate, to usurp power, to claim authorship."[18]

In addition, the double negative couplet *not...nor* (*ouk...oude*) is often used to link a thought together. The second negative usually confirms or strengthens the first. For example, in Romans 3:10 we read, "There is none [*ouk*] righteous, no not [*oude*] one."

Kroeger and Kroeger suggest that if we translate *authentein* as "to claim authorship" instead of "to have authority" the verse could legitimately read, "I do not allow a woman to teach nor to proclaim herself author of man."[19] I. Howard Marshall agrees: "It is therefore more likely that the verb [*authentein*] characterizes the nature of the teaching rather than the role of women in church leadership in general."[20] With this interpretation, the remaining verses correct the wrongful notion that woman was the author of man.

"For Adam was formed first then Eve" is the correct order of Genesis 2:7. However, being created first does not imply superiority, for if this is true, then birds of the air and fish of the sea would be superior to human beings since they were created prior.

"And Adam was not deceived." "A tenet of Gnosticism was that Adam was deceived, tricked into believing that he was born first."[21] But the correction is that he was not duped. "But the woman was deceived and became a transgressor." Again the Gnostic conten-

---

17. Kroeger and Kroeger, *I Suffer Not a Woman*, 81.
18. Ibid., 81–84.
19. Ibid., 103.
20. Witherington, *Women in the Ministry of Jesus*, 228.
21. Kroeger and Kroeger, *I Suffer Not a Woman*, 122.

tion was that Eve was superior to Adam and was without fault. The author of Genesis implicates both Adam and Eve; both were deceived by the serpent and banished from the garden.

"Yet she will be saved through childbearing, provided they continue in faith and love and holiness, with modesty." Much speculation has been made about the "she…they" of this verse and I will not enter into the debate. But once again a tenet of Gnosticism instructed women to abstain from childbearing and seek the more enlightened child-free path of salvation. Thus the Pastoral corrective is to affirm that childbearing is a noble thing and does not disqualify women from salvation "as long as they continue in faith, love, holiness and modesty."

John Wijngaards is not an ornithologist but rather a theologian. In one of his books, he writes about the birthing habits of the cuckoo bird.[22] It appears that cuckoo birds are fond of *laying* their eggs but not *hatching* their eggs. The practice of the cuckoo bird is this: after laying their eggs they look around for other bird nests that have similar eggs in regards to color and size (e.g., warblers, sparrows, wrens). When, for example, the warbler leaves her nest, the cuckoo bird places her egg in the nest of the warbler. The warbler returns and sits on the nest until all the eggs are hatched.

A strange thing happens when the cuckoo egg is hatched. The baby cuckoo bird begins finding and discarding the other birds and eggs within the nest. There is a tiny concave groove in the neck of the cuckoo bird that permits them to excavate objects in the nest. When the mother warbler returns to feed her babies, eventually there is only one large gapping mouth demanding food. The sad story is that the mother warbler keeps on feeding the intruder even though the much larger cuckoo bird is not her own.

When I read the cuckoo hatching account I had two insights. First, if I could speak bird fluently, I would say to all warblers, sparrows, and wrens, "GUARD YOUR NEST! Don't hatch and feed a slothful predator that places eggs in your nest. And do not feed the stranger that destroys your young. Guard your nest."

---

22. Wijngaards, *Ordination of Women*, 5.

The second insight is more of a metaphor for those traditions that have embraced women in leadership. GUARD YOUR PART-NERSHIP. Do not allow unexamined traditions to embed themselves into the thought life of the church. Rather, proactively and boldly affirm all persons as equally created in the image of God to lead. Remember, "So in Jesus Christ you are all children of God through faith, for all of you who were baptized into Christ have clothed yourself with Christ. There is neither Jew nor Greek, neither slave nor free, neither male nor female, for you are all one in Christ Jesus."[23]

Jennifer Gooch was an art student at Carnegie Mellon University. She is from south Texas and discovered northern winters to be extreme. During her first winter she observed many single lost gloves on the ground. She came to believe that a lone glove is useless without its mate. For her, "one lost glove" became a symbol for a sense of disconnect.

Out of her passion and creativity she developed a wall space in her apartment where these lost gloves could be displayed. A friend helped her to launch a website, www.onecoldhand.com, where lost gloves could be displayed. Her mission is to unite the lost and found. Her mission was born out of the value that "neither the loser nor the finder benefits." Two gloves are needed to function properly. Onecoldhand.com can be a reunion metaphor for women and men to reclaim their equal partnership in Christian ministry.

Admittedly, there are traditions in the Christian church that do not support women in leadership. My purpose is not to criticize or demonize. My purpose is to guard a theological position that traces its roots to creation and anchors its soul in Scripture, tradition, reason, and experience. I want to guard a truth that affirms leadership based on giftedness, not gender. I want to encourage the church to guard this partnership, not as a relic of the past, but as a reality for the future. The fields are white unto harvest, but workers are few. Whom shall we send to lead?

Women and men, guard your sacred partnership!

---

23. Galatians 3:26–28.

BIBLIOGRAPHY

Allison, Joseph D. "Heroines of the Faith." *Vital Christianity*, May 2, 1976, 12–14.

———. "The Life of D. S. Warner: Singing His Praises." *Vital Christianity*, December 1, 1974, 12–14.

Aristotle. *Nicomachean Ethics*. Translated by H. Rackhan. Cambridge, MA: Harvard University Press, 1956.

———. *Politics*. Translated by H. Rackham. New York: G. P. Putnam's Sons, 1932.

Balch, David L. "Early Christian Criticism of Patriarchal Authority: I Peter 2:11–3:12." *Union Quarterly Review* 39, no. 3 (1984).

———. "Hellenization / Acculturation in 1 Peter." In *Perspectives on First Peter*. Macon, GA: Mercer University Press, 1986.

———. *Wives Be Submissive: The Domestic Code of I Peter*. The Society of Biblical Literature Monograph Series, 26. Chicago: Scholars Press, 1981.

Barrett, C. K. *The First Epistle to the Corinthians*. Harper's New Testament Commentaries. New York: Harper & Row, 1968.

Bishop, Sarah, "Should Women Preach?" *Gospel Trumpet*, June 17, 1920, 9.

Bowers, Joyce M. "Roles of Married Women Missionaries: A Case Study." *International Bulletin of Missionary Research*, January 1984.

Brown, C. E. "Women Preachers." *Gospel Trumpet*, May 27, 1939, 9.

Bruce, F. F. *The Epistle to the Galatians*. The New International Greek Testament Commentary. Grand Rapids, MI: Wm. B. Eerdmans, 1982.

Byers, A. L. *The Birth of a Reformation, or the Life and Labors of Daniel S. Warner*. Anderson, IN: Gospel Trumpet, 1921.

———. "Pioneers of the Present Reformation: Sketch No. 3—Mary Cole." *Gospel Trumpet*, February 19, 1920, 22–23.

———. "Pioneers of the Present Reformation: Sketch No. 4—Sarah Smith." *Gospel Trumpet*, February 26, 1920, 5–6.

———. "Pioneers of the Present Reformation: Sketch No. 5—G. T. Clayton." *Gospel Trumpet*, March 4, 1920, 9–10.

———. "Pioneers of the Present Reformation: Sketch No. 12—Lodema Kaser." *Gospel Trumpet*, April 22, 1920, 5–6.

Caldwell, Dondeena. "Missionary? Wife? Or Both?" *Church of God Missions*, March 1988, 8.

———. "The Single Woman's Contribution to Missions." *Church of God Missions*, March 1988, 5–8.

Carroll, Jackson W., Barbar W. Hargrove. and Adair T. Lummis. "Women of the Cloth." *Grapevine,* November 2, 1982.

Casius, Dio. *Roman History*. Translated by Earnest Cary. New York: G. P. Putnam's Sons, 1917.

Catholic Biblical Association's Committee on the Role of Women. "Women and Priestly Ministry: The New Testament Evidence." *Catholic Biblical Quarterly* 41 (1979).

Clarke, Adam. *The Holy Bible...with a Commentary and Critical Notes*. 6 vols. New York: Abingdon, n.d.

Clear, Valoris B. *Where the Saints Have Trod: A Social History of the Church of God Reformation Movement*. Chesterfield, IN: Midwest Publications, 1977.

Cole, George L. Autobiography. In *A History of the Church: From the Birth of Christ to the Present Time*, compiled by Henry C. Wickersham, 345–52. Moundsville, WV: Gospel Trumpet Company, 1900.

[Cole, George L.] "The Labor of Women in the Gospel." *Gospel Trumpet*, December 28, 1905, 1.

Cole, Mary. *Trials and Triumphs of Faith*. Anderson: IN: Gospel Trumpet, 1914.

Crose, Lester A. *Passport for a Reformation*. Anderson, IN: Warner Press, 1981.

Davies, Eryl W. "Inheritance Rights and the Hebrew Levirate Marriage." *Vetus Testamentum* 31, no. 2 (April 1, 1981): 138–44. ATLA Religion Database.

Elliott, John H. *A Home for the Homeless: A Sociological Exegesis of I Peter, Its Solution and Strategy*. Philadelphia, PA: Fortress Press, 1981.

Engstrom, Ted W., and Edward R. Dayton. "The Best Man for the Job." *World Vision*, June–July 1988.

Fee, Gordon D. *1 & 2 Timothy, Titus*. New International Bible Commentary. Grand Rapids, MI: Baker Books, 2011.

Garcia, Gloria Salazar de. "Women's Ministries." *Latin America Pastoral Issues*, December 1987.

Glanville, Elizabeth. "Leadership Development for Women in Christian Ministry." PhD diss., Fuller Theological Seminary, 2000.

Gruber, Mayer. "The Status of Women in Ancient Judaism." In *Where We Stand: Issues and Debates in Ancient Judaism*, edited by Jacob Neusner and Alan J. Avery-Peck. Judaism in Late Antiquity, part 3, vol.2. Leiden, Netherlands: Brill Academic Publisher, 1999.

Hale, Mabel. "History of the Beginning and Early Years of the Church of God in Oklahoma City, OK." Unpublished manuscript. Anderson, IN: School of Theology Library, Anderson University.

Hardesty, Nancy A. *Women Called to Witness: Evangelical Feminism in the 19th Century*. Nashville, TN: Abingdon Press, 1984 (reprint Knoxville, TN: University of Tennessee Press, 1999).

Hardesty, Nancy, Lucille Sider Dayton, and Donald W. Dayton. "Women in the Holiness Movement: Feminism in the Evangelical Tradition." In *Women of Spirit: Female Leadership in the Jewish and Christian Traditions*, edited by Rosemary Ruether and Eleanor McLaughlin, 225–54. New York: Simon & Schuster, 1979.

Havelock, Ronald G. *The Change Agent's Guide to Innovation in Education.* Englewood Cliffs, NJ: Educational Technology Publications, 1973.

Hawkins, MaryAnn. "Church of God Clergywomen through the Lens of Leadership Emergence Theory." PhD diss., Fuller Theological Seminary, 2003.

Hiebert, Paul. "Phenomenology and Institutions of Folk Religions." Syllabus and lecture outlines. Pasadena, CA: Fuller Theological Seminary, 1986.

Hestenes, Roberta. "Is the Gospel Good News for Women?" *World Vision,* June/July 1988.

Hilcox, Edward. *The Star Book for Ministers.* Philadelphia, PA: Judson Press, 1906.

Huber, Randy. *Called, Equipped, No Place to Go.* Anderson IN: Warner Press/Church of God Ministries, 2003.

Jeremias, Joachim. *Jerusalem in the Time of Jesus.* Philadelphia, PA: Fortress Press, 1949.

Jewett, Paul K. *Man as Male and Female.* Grand Rapids, MI: Wm. B. Eerdmans, 1975.

Johnson, Alan F. *How I Changed My Mind about Women in Leadership.* Grand Rapids, MI: Zondervan, 2010. Kindle edition.

Kroeger, Catherine Clark, and Richard Clark Kroeger. *I Suffer Not a Woman.* Grand Rapids, MI: Baker Book House, 1992.

Lee, Luther. "Woman's Right to Preach the Gospel." In *Five Sermons and a Tract,* edited by Donald W. Dayton, 88–91. Chicago: Holrad House, 1975.

Loveland, Anne C. "Domesticity and Religion in the Antebellum Period: The Career of Phoebe Palmer." *Historian,* May 1977.

Malcolm, Karl Torjensen. *Women at the Crossroads: A Path Beyond Feminism and Traditionalism.* Downers Grove, IL: InterVarsity Press, 1982.

Martin, Ralph P. *Mark: Theologian and Evangelist.* Grand Rapids, MI: Zondervan, 1986.

———. *The Spirit and the Congregation.* Grand Rapids, MI: Wm. B. Eerdmans, 1984.

Massey, James Earl. *African Americans and the Church of God, Anderson, Indiana: Aspects of a Social History*. Anderson, IN: Anderson University Press, 2005.

Matthews, Victor, and Don C. Benjamin. *Social World of Ancient Israel: 1250–587 BCE*. Peabody, MA: Hendrikson, 1993.

McCutcheon, Lillie. "Lady in the Pulpit." *Centering on Ministry*. Anderson, IN: Center for Pastoral Studies, 1980.

Murphy, Cullen. "Women and the Bible." *Atlantic Monthly* 272, no. 2 (August 1, 1993): 39–45. ATLA Religion Database.

Myers, Carol L. "In the Household and Beyond: The Social World of Israelite Women." *Studia Theologica* 63, no. 1 (January 1, 2009): 19–41. ATLA Religion Database.

Neal, Hazel G., and Axchie A. Bolitho. *Madam President*. Anderson, IN: Gospel Trumpet, 1951.

Padgett, Alan. "Wealthy Women at Ephesus." *Interpretation* 41 (1989): 19–31.

Pagels, Elaine H. "Paul and Women: A Response to Recent Discussion." *AAR Presentation*. Chicago, 1974.

Palmer, Phoebe. *The Promise of the Father; or, A Neglected Specialty of the Last Days*. Boston: Henry V. Degen, 1859 (reprint, Salem, OH: Schmul, n.d.).

———. *The Way of Holiness*. 50th American ed., 1867 (reprint, Salem, OH: Schmul Publishing, 1988).

Plutarch. "Advice to a Bride and Groom." In Plutarch, *Moralia*, translated by Frank Cole Babbit, 297–343. New York: G.P. Putnam's Sons, 1928.

Raser, Harold E. *Phoebe Palmer: Her Life and Thought*. Lewiston, NY: Edwn Mellen Press, 1987.

Roberts, Benjamin T. *Ordaining Women*. Rochester, NY: Earnest Christian Publishing House, 1891 (reprint, Indianapolis, IN: Light and Life Press, 1992).

Rogers, Everett M., and Floyd F. Shoemaker. *Communication of Innovations: A Cross Cultural Approach*. 2nd ed. New York: Free Press, 1976.

Sanders, Cheryl James. *Ministry at the Margins: The Prophetic Ministry of Women, Youth and the Poor.* Eugene, OR: Wipf & Stock Publishers, 2009.

Sawyer, Sharon. "Women Pastors in the Church of God." *Colloquium* 8, no. 4 (July–August 1976).

Scholer, David M. "Women in Ministry." *The Covenant Companion,* December 1983–February 1984.

Shoffner, Lena. Autobiography. In *A History of the Church,* compiled by Henry C. Wickersham, 336–40. Moundsville, WV: Gospel Trumpet, 1900.

Smith, John W. V. *Heralds of a Brighter Day.* Anderson, IN: Gospel Trumpet Co. 1955.

———. *The Quest for Holiness and Unity.* Anderson, IN: Warner Press, 1980.

Smith, Sarah. Autobiography. In *A History of the Church,* compiled by Henry C. Wickersham, 301–13. Moundsville, WV: Gospel Trumpet, 1900.

———. "Fifty Years in the Kingdom of Heaven." *Gospel Trumpet,* January 21, 1892.

———. *Life Sketches of Mother Sarah Smith.* Anderson, IN: Gospel Trumpet, 1902.

Stanley, Susie. *Feminist Pillar of Fire: The Life of Alma White.* Cleveland, OH: Pilgrim Press, 1993.

———. "Galatians 3:28: Response." In *Women, Authority & the Bible,* edited by Alvera Mickelsen. Downers Grove, IL: InterVarsity Press, 1986.

———. *Holy Boldness: Women Preachers' Autobiographies and the Sanctified Self.* Knoxville, TN: University of Tennessee Press, 2002.

Stek, John. "Rahab of Canaan and Israel: The Meaning of Joshua 2." *Calvin Theological Journal* 37 (2002). ATLA Religion Database.

Stern, Rabbi. *Daily Prayers.* New York: Hebrews Publishing, 1928.

Vasholz, Robert I. "The Wisdom of Bathsheba in 1 Kings 2:13–25." *Presbyterion* 33, no. 1 (March 1, 2007): 49–318. ATLA Religion Database.

White, Alma. *The Story of My Life and Pillar of Fire*. Zarephath, NJ: Pillar of Fire, 1935–43.

———. *Woman's Ministry*. London: Pillar of Fire, [1921].

White, Charles. *The Beauty of Holiness*. Grand Rapids, MI: Francis Asbury Press, 1986.

Wijngaards, John. *The Ordination of Women in the Catholic Church*. New York: Continuum, 2001.

Williams, Lima Lehmer. *Walking in Missionary Shoes: A History of the Church of God in Kenya, East Africa (1905–1970)*. Anderson, IN: Warner Press, 1986.

Wilson, Bryan R. *Religious Sects*. New York: McGraw-Hill Books, 1970.

Witherington, Ben. *Women in the Ministry of Jesus*. New York: Cambridge University Press, 1984.

Wolff, Hans Walter. *Anthropology of the New Testament*. Philadelphia, PA: Fortress Press, 1974.

INDEX